The School of Patience

Discover Meaning in Suffering from the Life of Job

Joe Dickinson

Sermon To Book
www.sermontobook.com

The School of Patience / Joe Dickinson
ISBN-13: 978-1-952602-40-5

To my dear wife, Tisha, who has walked with me through dark days. To Jesus Christ, who led me and leads me.

CONTENTS

Welcome to the School of Patience

Be patient.

As a Christian, we know that "patience is a virtue." We know one of the fruits of the Spirit is "longsuffering" (Galatians 5:22)—which is synonymous with patience. James 1:2–3 tells us, "My brethren, count it all joy when ye fall into divers [various] temptations; knowing this, that the trying of your faith worketh patience."

Clearly, God values patience. But why? When I hear that Christians should be patient, I imagine myself sitting at a red light, waiting for the car ahead of me to finally make that right turn. Or I picture someone trying to coax a toddler to eat her supper. My understanding of situations in which I might need patience is limited to short periods of time when I might be mildly inconvenienced and annoyed.

But that's just the tip of the iceberg. There are far more serious situations in which we need to wait patiently while trusting our Heavenly Father. A man loses his job and struggles to find a new one. A woman hopes, month after month, that she will be able to conceive a child. Someone gets the news that they have a life-altering illness. When these seasons of difficulty come along, we need patience of an entirely different magnitude.

Furthermore, if waiting for a few minutes through irritating circumstances is my only understanding of what patience is all about, then I'm really missing out on the point of *biblical* patience. Not only that, but I will also lack this vital tool God created to help me when I go through the hardest times of my life.

Biblical Patience

Two people get ready to participate in a charity run. The first runner—let's call her Dana—stretches and then takes off running. She practices long-distance runs regularly. In her off time, she reads articles about improving her technique and listens to podcasts about how to manage each leg of the race.

Dan, the second runner, is not so prepared. He hasn't run for more than a few yards since he was a kid. Since Dan isn't familiar with proper running preparations, he ate too much for breakfast, isn't hydrated, and forgot to stretch.

It's not hard to guess which runner is going to give up, is it? Clearly, Dana is ready for this race. When she gets winded or has a cramp, she knows how to handle it. Even if her body tells her to quit, her mind is prepared and she's going to finish the race well. She can apply patience to these difficult parts, armed with mental strength and emotional tools to endure.

On the other hand, Dan is in trouble from the get-go. He might finish the first leg of the race, but he is completely unprepared for the greater hardship that comes further along. His body will tell him it's time to give up, and Dan will listen.

Patience in suffering is like running a race. When suffering comes, we typically don't have any choice but to just go through it. Those people who are trained in biblical patience will have the strength, stability, and contentment to endure cheerfully through whatever comes. Their worlds won't be destroyed; their faith won't crumble.

The School of Patience

When people think of Job from the Bible, the word *patience* often springs to mind. You've probably heard the phrase "the patience of Job." However, there's a lot more to Job's story. He didn't just wake up one morning, lose everything, and discover that he had a limitless source of patience to draw from.

God brought Job through a season of life that I like to call "the School of Patience." Suddenly, Job lost everything—his family, his wealth, his health, and his friends (Job 1–2). If Job had given up, no one would have blamed him. Yet God gently led him through the School of Patience, teaching Job lessons that grew his faith and enabled him to stand firm even when the worst happened.

And guess what? God wants to bring you through the School of Patience, too. Thankfully, you probably won't have to face the same trials Job did. Instead, you can examine Job's circumstances and learn the lessons God taught him so that you can be better prepared when you realize you're in the School of Patience.

Walking Through Suffering

Have you ever had dental work done? Whenever I need a filling, the dentist sits down and pulls out the big syringe. Then he warns me, "You're going to feel a little pinch." In short, he's letting me know that something uncomfortable is coming. When that pinch comes, I'm ready for it. I don't panic that the dentist is doing something unexpected and horrible. No, I can trust that he's doing what he said he would.

In the same way, God has told us very plainly that we will experience suffering in this life. Romans 8:18 tells us, "For I reckon that the sufferings of this present time are not worthy to be compared with the glory which shall be revealed in us." We will suffer now, but it won't compare with the glories God has planned for eternity.

Though we'll all experience suffering in this life, not every Christian goes through the School of Patience. From what I can tell, it's something God saves for people who are genuinely dedicated followers of Christ. Those who attend church on Sunday and don't give it another thought the moment they leave aren't invited to attend the School of Patience. You see, the School of Patience can teach you a lot, but it's not an easy journey. When trials come along, it takes devoted followers who cling tightly to God and have humble hearts to learn the lessons He has for them.

So, what should you do when you find yourself in a season of suffering? First off, know that suffering is to be expected. Just as the dentist warns you that discomfort is coming, God has warned you that suffering will come. Discomfort in your life is to be expected.

The Purpose of This Study

When life gets difficult, we can tend to turn angrily to God and demand, "Why do bad things happen to good people?" It's tempting to do that when we read the book of Job. Why *did* so many awful things happen to this good man and his family?

In Job's case, we do have part of the answer. In the first chapter of the book, we find God and Satan discussing Job. Satan asked if he could test Job, and God allowed it. It seems fairly straightforward.

But I want to throw this out there for consideration: besides the brief episode between God and Satan, the lengthy story of Job isn't really about why this happened to him. Job is never given an explanation. We and Job alike are left in the dark on the *why*. So I don't believe the main emphasis of Job's story is about why, but rather what. *Instead of "why bad things happen to good people," the book is about the good that God produces through the bad things.*

I don't know the source or cause of your suffering. There are many possible explanations—but when you're hurting or watching someone you love hurting, it's easy to get stuck on reasons and explanations.

This book offers another option. Instead of dwelling

only on why this is happening to you, I believe God would have you consider what He wants to accomplish in you through it. Isn't that exactly what James 1 says? Don't complain about the *why*, but rejoice in the *what*.

The School of Patience is about what God wants to develop *in you* as well as what He wants to teach you *about Him*. This book has two parts, accordingly. The first part will cover what I am going to call the *virtues* God wants to develop in you through the School of Patience. These are spiritual qualities or character traits that I believe will be exercised and developed in your spirit during your enrollment.

The second part will address the *wisdom and knowledge about God* that you will glean through the School of Patience. In other words, the second part addresses what you will learn about God and the nature of His wisdom.

At the end of each chapter, workbook sections will help you evaluate your life and apply the lessons of the School of Patience to your current exposure to suffering. And if you aren't currently suffering, learning about the School of Patience now will help you to be ready when the hard times inevitably arrive.

INTRODUCTION

The Trademarks of the School of Patience

Have you ever done a really tough weightlifting workout? If you do it right, by the time you're finished going through all your reps, you can hardly lift a finger. Your muscles have worked so hard that you couldn't do a single pushup. Your legs are wobbling, your head feels a little funny, and you struggle to stand up straight.

But if you have experience with this sort of thing, it doesn't faze you at all. Weightlifters know that this feeling of weakness actually means they are growing stronger. They understand this weird scientific phenomenon.

Going through spiritual struggles has a similar effect. You lost your job and have watched your savings drain away. Your wife is struggling with an ongoing medical condition. Your kids are inexplicably needy all of a sudden. In the midst of this storm, you feel like your faith has been shaken to its very core.

Instead of having a weightlifter's attitude, though, we

tend to think, "This is bad! I shouldn't be feeling this way! Shouldn't God be making things better? Things will never get better!" But the truth is that even though the pain of suffering feels bad, what it is building into you is good. A time of suffering in your life is another course in the School of Patience, and there are good things God wants to accomplish in you through it.

Job's Story

Most Christians are familiar with Job's story. Let me summarize the first two chapters briefly in case it's been a while since you last encountered the book of Job.

Job was an upstanding man. He had a large family, was wealthy and powerful, loved God, and had devoted friends. In fact, Job was doing so well in life that Satan approached God and asked if he might be allowed to test Job's devotion. For reasons beyond our limited human comprehension, God said yes.

Suddenly, Job started to lose everything. His children were killed. All of his sheep, oxen, camels, and donkeys were stolen or slaughtered. And to top it all off, Job was soon covered in painful sores.

That's when the rubber met the road. After all of that loss and pain, how was Job going to talk to God? Would he be angry, accusatory, or faithful? He didn't know it yet, but he'd been enrolled in the School of Patience.

Five Signs You're in the School of Patience

How do you know you've been enrolled in the School of Patience? Are you simply experiencing a brief bump in the road? Or is God really walking you through a difficult time in order to teach you something invaluable? I believe Job's story reveals some of the indicators that you're traveling through the School of Patience.

1. Suffering Without Explanation

The first characteristic of the school or patience is pain without explanation. This is one of Job's clearest indicators. Out of the blue, his children died, his property was destroyed, and his health was damaged. There's no good reason given for any of it—at least, not to Job.

Wouldn't it be nice if you came into a difficult stretch and God sat you down to show you in detail just why, exactly, He let the situation occur? Yes, it would be nice. But that isn't how God works. God wants His children to have a close enough relationship with Him to trust Him through all circumstances.

Job knew something big was at work. In Job 2:9, Job's wife told him to give up on God, but Job replied, "What? shall we receive good at the hand of God, and shall we not receive evil?" (Job 2:10b). Even though Job didn't know why these atrocities kept occurring, he knew that God was ultimately responsible for what was allowed to happen in his life.

When we face unexplained difficulties, may we respond like Job. I hope that I can continue walking in obedience, remembering that God has the right to walk us down an easy path or a hard path, depending on His good, loving purposes for us.

Rebelling against God. There are times when we experience suffering because of our own sin and rebellion. The story of Jonah comes to mind here. God asked Jonah to go to the dangerous Ninevites and tell them to repent (Jonah 1). Afraid, Jonah ran the other way. He then faced a number of hardships, until he finally came face to face with God in the belly of a whale and agreed to obey (Jonah 2).

When we hear that story, we tend to see him as weak in faith, but we have the same tendencies. Things don't go our way, so we throw up our hands, wondering where God is and why He isn't doing what we want. We are every bit as likely to quit and run toward sin as Jonah was.

Before you proceed, make sure that your suffering isn't due to your own sinful choices. If it is, the good news is that the solution is relatively simple: repent. Get right with God. Acknowledge your sin, ask forgiveness, and get back to living in obedience. First John 1:9 says, "If we confess our sins, he is faithful and just to forgive us our sins, and to cleanse us from all unrighteousness."

Suffering for no apparent reason. Perhaps much more vexing is when you know something is wrong, but you cannot put your finger on what it is. You just do not seem to have an explanation for why something difficult is happening to you. Like Job, you take hit after hit and can't figure out the reason for so much pain.

Suffering with no identifiable reason has a much more complex solution than repenting. In a nutshell, the answer is often to wait. Waiting—that isn't easy to do, is it? As hard as it is to believe while you're going through real pain, God has good reasons beyond our grasp for not always answering our prayers with a "yes" right away.

A young woman wanted to be married. She waited patiently year after year, hoping for a chance to find a good husband and start a family. After some time, she started to grow impatient, asking God why she had to wait so long. Finally, she met the man she ended up marrying and realized that, though she'd been ready to get married for years, her husband-to-be wasn't ready. He needed those years to work through things and find his way back to God.

Our timing is not anywhere near as good as God's timing. The School of Patience requires many classes in waiting, so prepare yourself to lean back and practice trusting God for the long haul. *Your goal is not to figure out why you are suffering, but what God wants you to learn from it.* David Jeremiah once said, "We waste a lot of time asking God, 'Why?' Because He most often doesn't let us see that part. So instead, start asking, 'What?' What do you want me to learn, Father?"[1]

2. Progressive Weakening of Faith

If you have been enrolled in the School of Patience, you might experience a weakening of your faith. No matter how strong your trust in God is, difficult seasons test you. There will be times when it is hard to keep holding on to the invisible promise that God does, indeed, have your best interests in mind.

Job experienced this very thing. In the first two chapters of Job, we see him standing strong even against his wife. But by the third chapter, Job began to bemoan being born. In Job 3:3 he said, "Let the day perish wherein I was born, and the night in which it was said, There is a man child conceived." From that point on, Job often questioned God's judgment and reasoning.

Perhaps one of the more frightening, yet common, experiences for an individual is when God begins to do a very intense work in the person's life and they find themselves becoming, in that moment, *weaker* in faith rather than stronger. If this is where you are, I want to encourage you: do not panic.

Remember the illustration of going to the gym and lifting weights. There are times when you have exercised your patience and faith to the point where they are exhausted. That's not a bad thing! What comes next is the ability to place your weary hand in God's and allow Him to take over. There is a new depth of love and trust that will be built through those times when you are at the end of what you can do.

3. Social Withdrawal

It's common for people who are experiencing difficult seasons to withdraw socially. When you are troubled deep in your soul, there are few people who can really help. Most want to give you encouragement, which in and of itself is a good thing. However, encouragement at the wrong time can seem shallow and dismissive.

Removing yourself from the company of others is one more sign that you might have been enrolled in the School of Patience. When you are dealing with things that few others understand, you will walk much of that path alone. You might find someone coming alongside you for short periods, but it is primarily a solitary journey.

Job 2:13 says, "So they sat down with him upon the ground seven days and seven nights, and none spake a word unto him: for they saw that his grief was very great." Three friends came and sat with him, yet they didn't speak. Not to mention, in the coming chapters, when they finally did speak, what they had to say wasn't very comforting. Even when you are surrounded by people, seasons of adversity can still isolate you.

4. Despairing of Life

When you go through periods of suffering, it is very common to think about how much easier it would be if you'd never been born. Job 3 goes into this lament in great detail. Verses 8 and 10 eloquently state, "Let them curse it that curse the day, who are ready to raise up their mourning.... Because it shut not up the doors of my mother's womb, nor hid sorrow from mine eyes." Job was wishing he weren't even alive.

Elijah felt the same way at one point. He was so discouraged that he asked God to take his life. He had just fought and won one of the greatest battles ever between good and evil. And yet, when it failed to bring the revival he thought it should have brought, he felt like a failure and wanted to die (1 Kings 19:4).

Now, let me be clear: I'm not saying that it's healthy to consider ending your life. If you are struggling with suicidal thoughts, you need to reach out to a pastor, friend, or counsellor immediately. Tell a trusted loved one and let this person get you the help you need.

However, wishing that suffering had never happened to you is a natural response. Suffering has a way of taking everything we know and flipping it upside down. The things we took for granted are yanked away, and we are left gasping for breath.

The point I want to get across is that you are not alone if you are despairing of life. This is not something to hide from God and feel ashamed of. Rather, go to Him freely and lament. Let Him comfort you in your pain and remind you of His enduring love for you. Though you despair of ever being born, God rejoices in you and is able to carry you through such times.

5. Feeling Lost or Trapped

I live two hours away from Carlsbad Caverns in New Mexico. This national park allows people to explore some of its one hundred caves. I have never experienced it, but during the tour, I'm told, everyone turns off their lights and gets to experience total darkness.

I can't imagine total darkness. Everywhere I've ever been has offered some pinprick of light. After a while, my eyes adjust, and I can usually make out shapes in the dark.

There are times during seasons of difficulties when we feel like we are in total darkness, lost in a maze of caves. Job 3:23 says, "Why is light given to a man whose way is hid, and whom God hath hedged in?" When we experience suffering, that line makes a lot of sense. What's the point of knowing there is a problem but not knowing how to solve it?

Sometimes, the problem can simply be that there are too many possible solutions. It's difficult to know which path is the right one when you're facing twenty different doorways. On the other hand, there are times when there are no possible solutions. You're imprisoned in your suffering, and no doorway is open to you.

I believe both of these are what James called, "divers temptations" (James 1:2) and also characteristics of the School of Patience. God has given us Job as a historic documentary of what the School of Patience looks like in a man's life. God does not leave us completely in the dark. I believe the book of Job is recorded because it reveals something to us about our God and Father: *He does not leave us completely in the dark even when He is leading us through the dark.* The experiences of Job are given to prepare us for the School of Patience, like that dentist saying, "All right, get ready. You are going to feel a little pinch."

Application

If you've been reading and now see that you are in the School of Patience, take heart. Though things seem dark, God has not left you alone. Here are some things to remember as you go forward:

1. Don't Panic

You will likely be tempted to panic when these symptoms begin to show up in your life. Panic will not help. In fact, it tends to only make things worse! This is, to me, one of the major reasons for a study like this book you're reading. It is intended to help you embrace suffering rather than panic in the midst of it.

If you know times of suffering are part of God's plan, you can take hope. You do not have to panic and say, "I need to quit church. I need to quit my marriage. I need to quit my job. I need to move. I need to do something crazy and drastic." No! Hang in there. Remember Job and know that suffering is part of the deal.

2. Count It Joy

As strange as this may sound, I implore you to rejoice. Thank God for what He is doing through this dark and difficult adversity you are experiencing. You might say, "Well, I don't know that I can do that." I want to encourage you to do it anyway. Again, James 1:2–3 tells us, "My brethren, count it all joy when ye fall into divers temptations; knowing this, that the trying of your faith worketh patience."

When I stop and thank God, even for my suffering, it helps remind me that though this tunnel is dark, it is leading somewhere good. You might not like the loud noise or the lack of light in that dark place, but you hold on to your seat because you know that God is using that tunnel to get you someplace where He can do good work in your life.

3. Endure

Blessed is the man that endureth temptation: for when he is tried, he shall receive the crown of life, which the Lord hath promised to them that love him.

—James 1:12

Hang in there. Do not quit. There is something better coming.

If you are in a place where all you can do is put one foot in front of the other, know that this is not necessarily a bad thing. Endure the monotony, the hardship, the endless days, knowing that one day you will share in God's glory.

When people get enrolled in the School of Patience, one of two things happens: either they give up and quit, or they buckle their seatbelts and hold tight for the ride to come. Those who give up can waste years running from God. But those who cling tighter to God get to experience incredible blessings.

I hope that learning about the School of Patience will help prepare you for the next time God takes you by the hand and says, "All right, we are going through a tunnel now." That you won't panic but, like a small child, you will follow your Heavenly Father wherever He leads, trusting that He won't let you be lost in the dark.

WORKBOOK

Introduction Questions

Question: Have you experienced seemingly inexplicable suffering in your life? Evaluate your situation and ask the Holy Spirit to reveal if you have walked in any disobedience that has led you into this place of difficulty. If so, repent and return to a place of obedience. If not, surrender your heart before God to wait patiently on Him.

_____

_____

_____

_____

_____

_____

_____

_____

_____

Question: Review the five signs of being in the School of Patience: suffering without explanation, progressive weakening of faith, social withdrawal, despairing of life, and feeling lost or trapped. Which, if any, of these characteristics describe your current situation? Consider whether you need to shift your perspective from asking, "Why?" to asking, "What does God want me to learn from this?"

_____

_____

_____

_____

_____

_____

_____

_____

_____

_____

Question: What have been your thoughts toward or about God during times of difficulty (past or present)? Does knowing that God has a plan for bringing you through the School of Patience change how you view and feel about the circumstances you are walking through? How so?

_____

_____

_____

_____

_____

_____

_____

_____

_____

_____

Action: As God brings you through the School of Patience, it is important to set your focus to 1) overcome panic, 2) count it all joy, and 3) walk with endurance. Find Bible verses that help you maintain the perspectives in each of those three points. Get three pieces of paper and write down the titles "Don't Panic," "Count It All Joy," and "Endure," respectively. Then write the corresponding Bible verses on each paper. Display them to remind yourself of those verses in times of trouble.

Introduction Notes

_____

_____

_____

_____

_____

_____

_____

_____

_____

_____

_____

_____

_____

_____

_____

_____

_____

_____

_____

_____

_____

_____

_____

Part One:
Virtues Developed in the School
of Patience

CHAPTER ONE

A Proper Paradigm for Problems

The end of Job 2 tells us that three of Job's friends showed up. Eliphaz, Bildad, and Zophar heard about Job's string of unfortunate events and came to see how they could help. But they weren't prepared for the reality of the depths of Job's misery. In fact, as we've seen, they were so shocked by what they found that "they sat down with him upon the ground seven days and seven nights, and none spake a word unto him: for they saw that his grief was very great" (Job 2:13).

At first, this made me think that these three friends really understood what Job was going through. What sensitive guys! Surely, they truly got what was going on and would be a great comfort to their friend. I'm sorry to say, that isn't how it played out. You see, these men were operating under some faulty beliefs about suffering. Since they didn't have a proper paradigm for problems, their advice was doomed to miss the mark.

Remember, the School of Patience isn't so much about why problems come, but about what God wants to accomplish in us through them. There are a number of spiritual virtues that God wants to imbue in us through the School of Patience. Chapters One through Five of this book will explore these virtues, starting with the first: we need a new paradigm for problems. *Paradigm* is the way you look at things, or your point of view. So when I say we need a new paradigm, I mean we need to make sure we are looking at problems from the proper perspective.

Eliphaz's Reproof

Let's examine precisely what Eliphaz said to Job. Remember, these men had been sitting with their friend in silence for seven days. They had plenty of time to witness Job's suffering and come up with their very best advice.

In chapter 3, recall that Job lamented ever being born. He poured out his misery, and now Eliphaz was going to say something to point Job toward better things. Unfortunately, what Eliphaz essentially said was, "You are suffering because you've done something wrong. This is your fault, and you need to make things right with God." Look at Job 4:7: "Remember, I pray thee, who ever perished, being innocent? or where were the righteous cut off?"

And to make things worse, Eliphaz said in Job 5:17: "Behold, happy is the man whom God correcteth: therefore despise not thou the chastening of the Almighty." Not only did Eliphaz think this was all Job's fault, but he also admonished Job to be grateful for it.

Now, there are some definite biblical truths there. We are to be grateful and rejoice. But when we see that all of

Job's children died, his wife told him to give up on God, his livelihood was destroyed, and he was covered in terrible sores, those words seem rather cruel.

Have you ever had someone give you unhelpful advice in the midst of your suffering? Even if the words are true, they aren't necessarily the right ones to say at that time. In fact, well-intentioned words can add to our suffering.

When we are being crushed by hardship, we need to correct two major misconceptions: first, that we are not the only people who have suffered; second, that problems are somehow unfair. We can't hear the truth when we're so busy believing lies about suffering.

Misconception #1 About Suffering: You Are All Alone

"Nobody understands what I'm going through." Have you ever heard yourself say that? When it comes to the people surrounding you, you might be right. Even if you know that others have gone through similar things, it's easy to feel very alone in your specific suffering.

I think that's a very common feeling as we go through experiences that are molding and shaping us. Feeling that no one else can understand our suffering is likely an exaggeration, but it is a very real sensation.

Think of Jesus as He was in the Garden of Gethsemane (Matthew 26:36–45). He took a few disciples along and asked them to pray. While Jesus was sweating blood, knowing full well what agony was on its way, His dearest friends fell asleep. How alone Jesus must have felt!

After His arrest, Jesus' disciples got scared and ran

(Matthew 26:56). Then, on the cross, God Himself turned away from Jesus. Before He died, Jesus cried, "My God, my God, why hast thou forsaken me?" (Matthew 27:46).

When you are in the middle of a season of suffering, know that Jesus Christ understands exactly how alone you feel. Despite how you may feel in the moment, because Jesus suffered alone, believers never will.

In fact, removing or distancing the most supportive people from your life can be a way that God develops your dependence on Him. You're in the midst of a painful experience and your dearest friends suddenly have nothing helpful to say, or your family members become wrapped up in their own lives. I think it's possible that God sometimes strips us of our usual go-to people so that we have nowhere else to turn but Him.

Talking with a mentor, a friend, or your spouse isn't a bad thing. But there are times when even those closest to you can't really understand what's going on in your life. And that's perfectly normal. After all, the only one who can possibly know everything you go through is God. When you find yourself feeling alone in your suffering, it's time to draw near to Jesus Christ and let Him remind you that you are not alone.

Misconception #2 About Suffering: It's Unfair

It's tempting for us modern-day American Christians to believe that if we are faithful to God, He will reward us with easy lives. I myself have experienced times when life was going along just fine, but then something came out of left field and I start telling God how unfair it was for me to have to go through any sort of difficulty.

So that my soul chooseth strangling, and death rather than my life. I loathe it; I would not live [always]: let me alone; for my days are vanity. What is man, that thou shouldest magnify him? and that thou shouldest set thine heart upon him? And that thou shouldest visit him every morning, and try him every moment? How long wilt thou not depart from me, nor let me alone till I swallow down my spittle?
—Job 7:15–19

It's interesting that when you come to church, you can get this impression that Christians are supposed to have an attitude like, "Rah rah rah! God is good! We're all happy Christians!" And yes, God *is* good. But our current culture hasn't given us the ability to remember that hard seasons will come and that it's perfectly okay when they do.

Even though it's normal to feel that experiencing suffering is unfair, we need to be careful not to fall into sin. We must watch our thought patterns carefully so that we don't start making assumptions about God. It's all too easy to start imagining that God is out to get us or has turned away. We might even be tempted to believe that these struggles are due to an unforgiving, uncaring, capricious God.

When God is developing patience in a man or woman's life, we may experience times when it seems like God is unjust or unfair. The School of Patience will challenge your belief about God's presence, His love, and His fairness.

That's why it's time to change our paradigm about suffering. We like to believe that when we are being obedient, God rewards us with good health, success at work, more money, and great relationships. That's a house-of-cards kind of faith. An easy life is not an indicator of God's love for you. It's possible that God allows you to go through a season of struggle in order to start stripping away those misconceptions. It's also possible that He has some other reason, which He isn't going to explain to you, to allow these difficulties in your life.

Believe it or not, suffering can be completely unrelated to whether or not you've been obeying God. Being angry that this season is "unfair" is immature. Regardless of why God has allowed this hardship in your life, He will use the School of Patience to knock down faulty beliefs about suffering and build a new paradigm that is true and sturdy.

Application

1. You Are Not Alone

No matter how distant your loved ones might feel during this season of life, remember that you are not the only person ever to experience such things. Spend some time reading through the Psalms. There you will find other people who are crying out to God in the midst of difficult times. Remember that God can use your current pain to equip you to help others down the road not to feel alone.

2. Remember the Cross

God Himself knows what it's like to suffer and to be abandoned and betrayed. Jesus was tempted in every way (Matthew 4) but never sinned. Read Matthew 5:1–11 and meditate on the blessings that Jesus says exist for those who are downtrodden. And never forget that Jesus' cruel suffering on the cross means that one day this life will come to an end and you will get to be with God in heaven for all eternity. Our suffering has an expiration date (Romans 8:17–18).

3. Set Your Eyes on Heavenly Things

It's tempting to get so focused on our problems that we can't see anything or anyone else. Our world shrinks down to ourselves and our struggles. That isn't how God wants us to live. We might have seasons in which we need to take care of ourselves, but then we are to return to caring for our neighbors. Never are we to give up loving the people around us.

4. Remember That God Is in Control

It might not feel like it, but the God of the universe is not in heaven wringing His hands and fretting over how your life has turned out. His plan for your life might not be at all what you wanted for yourself. However, as you learn to trust in Him while you wait and endure through the dark times, you can discover a wealth of good things you never before knew could occur.

Let me remind you of something James said: Count it all joy. If you need wisdom, ask for it (James 1:5). Hang in there. Blessed are those of us who endure—there is a crown of life waiting for us (James 1:12).

WORKBOOK

Chapter One Questions

Question: *Have you ever had someone give you unhelpful advice in the midst of your suffering?* Why do you think their advice wasn't helpful? Compare and contrast their advice to principles found in God's Word.

_____

_____

_____

_____

_____

_____

_____

_____

_____

_____

Question: *When you are in the middle of a season of suffering, know that Jesus Christ understands exactly how alone you feel.* Have you experienced feelings of isolation and loneliness during difficult times? Is it your automatic reaction to turn to God or to others when you're struggling? Do you think God is using your loneliness to provide you with the opportunity to come to Him?

_____

_____

_____

_____

_____

_____

_____

_____

_____

_____

Question: *Even though it's normal to feel that experiencing suffering is unfair, we need to be careful not to fall into sin.* In your humanness, what thoughts and feelings have come to the surface amid your suffering? Have you crossed the line and entered into a sinful place in any of those thoughts or feelings? Have you found yourself embracing false assumptions about the character of God? If so, take some time before God to confess and repent.

_____

_____

_____

_____

_____

_____

_____

_____

_____

_____

_____

Action: It's easy to become introspective and self-serving during times of suffering. However, reaching out to love and serve others even in the midst of your own pain can be another kind of healing balm. It is important to keep your mind focused on heavenly things. Think of someone in your life who would be blessed by a personal act of kindness. Create a plan for how to reach out to that person in the next week or two. Keep your heart turned to God as you serve the other person. Write about the experience and what God showed you through it.

Chapter One Notes

_____

_____

_____

_____

_____

_____

_____

_____

_____

_____

_____

_____

_____

_____

_____

_____

_____

_____

_____

_____

_____

_____

_____

CHAPTER TWO

Christ-Centered Faith

Forest fires are devastating, aren't they? We all know this. After all, Smokey the Bear informed us from a young age that we are the ones who can prevent them! And anyone who's seen Disney's movie *Bambi* has firmly imprinted the image of innocent animals running from the fiery inferno.[2]

But did you know that sequoia trees actually need fire in order to reproduce? These giant trees are native to California and survive wildfire season after wildfire season. The flames actually strengthen their bark. There are a number of other trees with serotinous cones, which are sealed with a resin that only burns away during a forest fire. In other words, these trees can't reproduce without fire.

Not only that, but wildfires benefit forests by burning away brush that's collected on the floor. Once that dried-up debris is out of the way, new growth can occur. Old, dead trees eaten up by bugs are safely destroyed by the flames. The soil is made richer.

Some time ago, the forest rangers in our national parks were extremely diligent in stamping out forest fires as soon as they sprang up. However, as time went by, they realized that this was actually preventing the forests' natural growth. The forests were less healthy because fires weren't blazing through. Controlled fires were, in fact, vital to keeping the trees strong.

It's not hard to see the analogy between forest fires and the difficult seasons of our lives. We like to fill our lives with all kinds of things—some good, some not so good. Hard times have a way of rushing through all parts of our lives and clearing out the debris we've collected. They let us have space to grow new, healthy practices. They hurt, but they strengthen.

The difficulty lies in being able to see the benefit of our painful circumstances when we're in the middle of them. Like the sequoia tree in the midst of that eight-hundred-degree fire, when we are going through excruciating situations, we aren't instinctively thinking, "This is uncomfortable, but it sure is going to make me stronger when it's done!"

In fact, when you're in the midst of one of life's forest fires, what comes naturally is doubting God's goodness. Without the virtue of centering our faith on Christ, it can't help but crumble in the searing heat.

Bildad's Accusations

According to Job 8, Bildad jumped in and gave Job some advice. Like Eliphaz before him, Bildad was quick to blame Job for the misfortunes that beset him. In verse

6, Bildad said, "If thou wert pure and upright; surely now [God] would awake for thee, and make the habitation of thy righteousness prosperous."

Remember in the beginning of the book of Job where God Himself said that Job was upright and perfect (Job 1:8)? If God saw this in Job, surely his friends saw what a good man he was.

With that in mind, Bildad's reproof takes on a new light. Telling Job that he must be the root cause of his own suffering is as ridiculous as telling the sequoia trees that it's their fault the lightning struck the ground and started the fire.

Yet it's our human nature to be quick to assign blame. We can't seem to accept that lightning and forest fires naturally occur. We live in a fallen, sinful world where hardship is an unavoidable part of the equation. Jobs are lost, friends betray our trust, and terrible things happen to those we love. While some of these things can be caused by human choices, assigning blame is often misleading.

Though Job knew this on some level and tried to defend himself in chapter 9, he had thrown up his hands in frustration by chapter 10. Job 10:14–19 lays out his despair:

If I sin, then thou markest me, and thou wilt not acquit me from mine iniquity. If I be wicked, woe unto me; and if I be righteous, yet will I not lift up my head. I am full of confusion; therefore see thou mine affliction; for it increaseth. Thou huntest me as a fierce lion: and again thou shewest thyself marvellous upon me. Thou renewest thy witnesses against me, and increasest thine indignation upon me; changes and war are against me. Wherefore then hast thou brought me forth out of the womb? Oh that I had given up the ghost, and no eye had seen me! I should have been as though I had not been; I should have been carried from the womb to the grave.

The question then becomes: what are we to do when we are in the middle of one of life's forest fires? How do we take our natural responses and let God refine them into virtues?

Frustration: When Your Best Isn't Enough

Frustration is a natural response to difficult seasons of life. When we realize that God is leading us through the School of Patience, we rarely jump for joy. Rather, when we begin to see clearly just how helpless we are in our situation, frustration inevitably sets in.

You can hear Job's frustration in Job 9:13–14: "If God will not withdraw his anger, the proud helpers do stoop under him. How much less shall I answer him, and choose out my words to reason with him?" Job was righteous before God, yet he felt that God was punishing him for something he'd done. I can only imagine how Job must have pleaded with God, pointing out that he was, in fact, blameless. Still the trials kept on coming. No wonder he was frustrated!

I've seen this frustration, particularly in Christians who are still young in their faith. We seem to believe that if we are faithful to God and start putting right practices in place that we will be exempted from hardship. No sooner do we stamp out this fire then we turn the corner and find another

THE SCHOOL OF PATIENCE · 43

one has sprung up. And all this struggling reveals a lot of ugliness in our hearts.

Helplessness:
When You Can't Do Better Than Your Best

Have you ever seen the old Disney cartoon *Cinderella*?[3] Poor Cinderella was beautiful, kind, and had a lovely singing voice. She was downtrodden by her stepmother and stepsisters, forced to work long hours as a servant in the very house she grew up in as a cherished daughter. Finally, after years of such terrible treatment, a fairy godmother appeared to reward Cinderella's goodness. The handsome prince recognized her as a treasure and married her, making her a princess and reversing all of the terrible things that had happened to her.

When we go through painful circumstances, there's a temptation to expect to have our own Cinderella stories. At first, we go politely to God and point out all the things we've done right, as though we expect Him to say, "Sorry! I meant for this suffering to be visited on the fellow next to you. Never mind!" Or else we hope that He'll give us generous restitution for the hardships we've endured.

And while God does, indeed, have a plan to swoop in and end our suffering through Christ, it rarely happens the way we expect. It doesn't take long for us to grow tired of pleading our cases before God. Soon, our frustration is exhausted—and in its place, we experience *helplessness*.

Read what Job 9:16–17 says: "If I had called, and he had answered me; yet would I not believe that he had hearkened unto my voice. For he breaketh me with a tempest, and multiplieth my wounds without cause." Job's hands were thrown up in the air because he had done his best, yet his character was still being assaulted.

Why would God allow such a seemingly fruitless frustration? Well, why are forest fires helpful? They burn off things that really shouldn't be there, to make room for things that should. In our case, it may be that God is burning off our tendency to lean on our own merits and performance, to make room for something better. Like what?

Jesus, Our Mediator

The next lesson to be learned is that rather than wallow in helpless frustration, we must begin to trust our mediator, Jesus Christ. In 1 John 2:1b, Paul told us "And if any man sin, we have an advocate with the Father, Jesus Christ the righteous."

Imagine that you have been accused of a terrible crime. After being booked, you've sat in jail worrying until the day of your arraignment. Hands cuffed together, the bailiff brings you into the courtroom where the judge, God Himself, sits. You stand before Him, knowing full well that you are a guilty sinner. He reads the charges against you and says, "How do you plead?"

All of a sudden, the door opens, and in strides Jesus. Confidently, He comes to stand at your side and announces, "I represent this person." Then Jesus proceeds to mediate on your behalf. In no time, God bangs His gavel and declares you free to go.

Any time we face the overwhelming accusation that

God is allowing trouble to befall us because of our sin, we must remember that we have a mediator. Jesus defends us, not by our merit or performance, but by His.

No matter how well we first understood our utter dependence on Christ's salvation, there is still something inside us that makes us believe we have to do more, do better, be perfect. It's almost as though we envision some heavenly reward system based on our achievement points. When disaster strikes, we panic and assume that we haven't "leveled up" enough to earn an easy life.

I want to turn that thinking on its head. What if it is only when we are praying, reading our Bible, tithing, fasting, and serving that God chooses to allow us to be led into the School of Patience? That was true in Job's case, wasn't it? Because he was so devout, God believed he could withstand so many trials. Perhaps God leads us to difficult situations with the plan of teaching us a number of important lessons. He allows the lightning to strike in order to burn up the debris on our forest floors, so to speak.

And as we allow the distractions in our lives to fade away, we have more room for Jesus. It is only when we realize how very helpless we are to save ourselves that we accept Him in the first place. Maybe we need periodic reminders that we still rely upon Christ for so much.

Does that mean I should stop reading my Bible and praying? If I leave God alone, will He leave me alone? By no means! But let's realign our purpose for spiritual discipline. We spend time with God because we delight in Him and eagerly desire to be more like Him. We don't read our Bibles because we hope God looks down on us and awards us our well-earned points. We're not checking things off a spiritual scavenger hunt list, hoping to turn it in for a prize. Rather, we joyfully make space in our lives to spend quality time with our beloved Father.

Are you in the School of Patience? Are you frustrated and feeling helpless? If so, don't panic. Remember the dentist's warning: you're going to feel a pinch. When you find yourself frustrated with suffering, it's time to fix your eyes on the cross. When you feel helpless, you must remember that Jesus is busy mediating on your behalf.

The greatest resource God has given to mankind is His Son, Jesus Christ. He is the way, the truth, and the life (John 14:6). He is the vine; we are the branches (John 15:5). He is the bread of life. He is the water of life. He is the light of life. Depend on Jesus, not only for your salvation, but for every step that comes after, as well.

Application

1. Stop!

First of all, stop. Stop trying to force something to happen. You can't manipulate God into doing what you want. Stop trusting in your own ability to fix everything. Stop depending on your own performance and your own merits as a way to somehow try to earn God's favor, help, and blessing. Remember, your righteousness is like filthy rags to God (Isaiah 64:6)! So stop trying to use it as a bargaining chip with Him. God is trying to "burn up" your faith in *you* to make room for more faith in *Christ*.

2. Start Depending on God's Mercy

He promises to provide for His children. It might not happen the way you want or in your chosen timeframe, but God is faithful. Whenever you start to believe that your problems are a result of your sin, remember the freedom Jesus gave us on the cross. Your sins are forgiven. That doesn't give us license to sin as much as we want. Rather, it means that God has traded Jesus' righteousness for your sinfulness.

3. Trust in Jesus Alone

Remember that one of the lessons in the School of Patience is that we must stop putting our hope and trust in anything but Jesus. That wildfire is going to rip through your life and demolish your ability to trust in yourself and your resources. All the other things on which you've centered your faith are revealed to be shaky and disappointing. Only Jesus is worth centering our faith upon.

WORKBOOK

Chapter Two Questions

Question: Take an honest look at your life. How is the suffering you're experiencing clearing the way for new growth? What things need to be burned away in order to allow this new growth to emerge?

_____

_____

_____

_____

_____

_____

_____

_____

_____

_____

_____

Question: When you find yourself experiencing difficulty, are you quick to assign blame to explain what's happening to you? Who or what do you usually blame? Why do you think you try to find a reason for your suffering?

_____

_____

_____

_____

_____

_____

_____

_____

_____

_____

Question: Do you find yourself worrying that when things go wrong in your life, it's because you've done something wrong, or because God isn't happy with you? What does God's Word say about that worry? Is it possible that you may be going through this situation _because_ you are in a good place with God? How does that possibility affect your perspective on your current situation?

_____

_____

_____

_____

_____

_____

_____

_____

_____

_____

_____

Action: *Whenever you start to believe that your problems are a result of your sin, remember the freedom Jesus gave us on the cross.* If the suffering in your life has filled you with fear and doubt that you aren't doing enough to "earn" favor from God, then take a minute to remind yourself that your standing with God is based on the finished work of Jesus on the cross. Find a worship song that communicates this truth and spend some time connecting with God through worship.

Chapter Two Notes

CHAPTER THREE

Empathy

Do you know what I love to eat? Brownies fresh from the oven with a big scoop of really good vanilla ice cream. My mouth starts watering just reading that sentence. When the ice cream melts and gets soaked up by the warm brownie, it is just about the most delicious thing ever.

Now, if I love that dessert, why would I stop eating it? What would it take for me to refuse it if my wife served it to me one night after supper? Well, I might be on a diet. If I needed to lose weight or get my blood sugar under control, I might not indulge in my favorite dessert. If we had company over and discovered that we were one serving short, I would give up my portion to one of my guests. It would take a really good reason, but there are situations in which I would forgo brownies and ice cream.

Similarly, what does it take for people to make other sacrifices in life? Going to the gym is painful and expensive, but that doesn't stop us from making it part of our routines. Running in 90-degree heat, hiring a trainer to push us to the breaking point, or riding a bike through the pouring rain all sound pretty awful. So, why do we do these things? We do them because we know that they serve a good purpose in strengthening our bodies.

We're willing to endure pain now with the knowledge that it will pay off later. This is why people go through financial seminars and make drastic budget cuts in order to get out of debt. They suffer without the luxuries now so that they can enjoy them (more) later.

And that is exactly the same way we can go through the School of Patience without despairing. When we understand that God has good things to teach us, we can walk through these hard times and still trust in our Heavenly Father.

Remember, again, what James 1:2–3 tells us: "My brethren, count it all joy when ye fall into divers temptations; knowing this, that the trying of your faith worketh patience." It's worth not going out to eat right now, because it'll help us pay off our student loans faster. In the same way, it's worth walking faithfully with God as my mom goes through breast cancer treatment, because of what God is developing in my life through that experience.

The next virtue we're going to discuss is empathy. One of the quickest lessons we learn in the School of Patience is how to empathize with others who are going through the same situations we are. You'd think that going through hardship would make us great empathizers. And while we all feel empathy, we don't always put it to good use.

Being a Better Friend

Do you know who was terrible at comforting a friend in need? Eliphaz and Bildad, two of Job's cohorts. I mean, these two men sat with Job for seven whole days, listening to his grief. They saw his sores. They'd spoken to his children who died. They saw his flocks in the fields before they were stolen away. Eliphaz and Bildad were in the perfect place to offer loving comfort to Job.

And they disappointed Job thoroughly.

Of course, if you haven't gone through a long illness yourself, you don't really know what it's like. If you haven't lost a child, you can't imagine the grief. If you haven't lost your job and watched your life savings disappear, you don't understand the fear that comes along with that. Without your own suffering, you can only offer so much empathy.

Still, I think we can all agree that it's a bad idea to sit with a friend after his debilitating car accident and tell him his legs are in traction because he's a sinner. Going to a funeral and telling the wife of the deceased that her husband is dead because of some sort of sin is absolutely the wrong thing to do. We know this, yet there is often a temptation for us to place unhelpful blame.

On the other hand, Proverbs 25:11 says, "A word fitly spoken is like apples of gold in pictures of silver." *The right words at the right time are life-giving.* They offer true comfort and emotional release. Sometimes, just asking what it's like to live with chronic pain, and then really listening to the answer, allows a friend to reveal the hurt she has to keep hidden. Asking the bereaved to tell stories of the lost loved one lets a friend remember the life that was lived rather than the emptiness of the loss.

And reminding our hurting friends that God will never leave nor forsake them doesn't dismiss or downplay their pain. Rather, it allows them to know that they are not alone, without offering platitudes that actually make the hurting feel lonelier than ever.

The Empathy of Christ

Jesus experienced a wide spectrum of suffering while on earth. Before He began His ministry, He fasted for forty days and was tempted in every way possible. His neighbors, family members, and friends rejected Him, causing Him to say, "A prophet is not without honour, save in his own country, and in his own house" (Matthew 13:57). His mother and brothers came to bring Him home and make Him stop ministering (Mark 3:31–32). Jesus' disciples didn't understand Him, and bickered over their place in the Kingdom of God (Mark 10:37–45; Luke 22:24–30). They abandoned Him in His moment of need (Mark 14:50).

The religious leaders and the political leaders of the day all rejected Jesus (Luke 23:35). He was betrayed by the people He had come to save (John 1:11; Luke 22:47–48; Luke 23:21). He suffered physically; He was tortured and killed brutally (John 19). Even God Himself turned His back on Jesus (Matthew 27:46).

What is really poignant about all this suffering is that Jesus deserved none of it. If suffering must be earned, Jesus should have been exempt for life. Yet He entered into this world willingly and suffered terribly, knowing the eternal good He was achieving (John 10:17–18).

First Peter 2:21 tells us, "For even hereunto were ye called: because Christ also suffered for us, leaving us an example, that ye should follow his steps." Peter makes it clear that we are going to suffer, too. In fact, suffering is a mark of the followers of Christ.

Have you ever gone on a mission trip to a developing country? Something remarkable happens when Christians suffer together for the gospel. When we go out in obedience and live through difficult circumstances with our fellow believers, we are forever bonded in brotherhood.

Going through the School of Patience gives us an opportunity to bond with Jesus Christ. We can develop a deeper appreciation for His suffering and His perfect response to it. We can take comfort from knowing that we are not alone in our pain. These difficult seasons should drive us deeper into reading the Word and praying.

When our loved ones are going through their own difficult seasons, our empathetic response is to encourage them toward a closer relationship with Jesus. Praying and studying the Bible together can strengthen the bonds between the sufferer and Christ, as well as between the sufferer and you.

We are to "count it joy" when we go through hardships. That doesn't mean we are happy about it. Rather, we have the maturity to have joy in the closeness to our Savior that we are about to experience. When our friends experience pain and suffering, we can pray that they, too, will let this season build their faith and our friendship.

Application

1. Encourage Someone

Unless you are a hermit on a mountaintop, you know someone who is going through some sort of difficulty. First of all, take the time to be aware of those around you enough that you can recognize when a loved one is suffering.

Then, take the time to encourage that person. Even if you aren't certain that this person is having a hard time, an encouraging word can still be life-giving. As you grow in your ability to hear the Holy Spirit's promptings, you'll find more and more ways to encourage those around you.

When you read your Bible, be aware of verses that are particularly meaningful to you. Ask God who else might need to hear that verse. Send off a quick text to that person with the verse and a loving message.

Encourage someone by listening. Ask thoughtful questions and really listen when the person responds. Learn the difference between listening and commiserating. Don't answer with, "I lost my job once, too. Here's the whole story of my suffering." Instead, try, "I lost my job once, too. It really shook my sense of self. Your boss has lost a great salesman. You are such a charismatic person."

Call your friend to say that he was on your mind and you prayed for him. Invite the friend to spend time doing something together, even if it's just sitting and watching the football game or going to McDonald's for lunch. Let him know that his pain has not escaped your notice, and when the time is right, remind him that his pain has not escaped God's notice.

Avoid giving advice. Talking through possible options and having an opinion on which is best is one thing. Telling the person what to do is a great way to make your friendship obsolete. You are not in this person's shoes. You are not God. You do not need to be the person who does most of the talking.

2. Spend Time with Jesus

Remember when I said that Jesus knows what it's like to suffer? Well, it's not enough just to know that about Him. Having Him live in your house and never once talking to Him doesn't count as spending time together. You have to actually get up out of your seat, walk over, and sit in His presence.

And, you know what? It's okay to lay your heart bare. Tell Him you are struggling to have faith through all of this. Confess the things that are hard for you to trust. Explain what you think you need from God. In short, surrender all of it to Him.

An amazing thing happens when we are honest with God. We stop holding on to all our heavy baggage and, instead, entrust it to Him. The baggage still needs to be dealt with, but we aren't trying to carry it alone.

Read the Gospels and pay attention to Jesus' suffering—and His response to it. Spend time looking at the Psalms, particularly those laments that describe suffering.

Don't waste time feeling guilty or worrying that you are a "bad" Christian. Remember that Jesus suffered. He went to God in the Garden of Gethsemane and asked for the heavy load to be removed from Him. It's okay to tell God that you are afraid, that the road you're traveling seems impossible, and that you feel abandoned. Jesus experienced those same feelings and was sinless. The more time you spend getting to know Him, the better prepared you'll be to follow in His perfect footsteps.

3. Embrace This Difficult Season

What do you do when you know a storm is coming? I'm talking about a huge storm like a hurricane or a blizzard. You prepare for it, don't you? You get the outside of your house ready. You stock up supplies. Then you hunker down and wait it out.

Believe it or not, there is incredible blessing to be found in the midst of adversity. You spend more time with God, pouring out your heart and asking for help. You simplify your life, cutting out the extra things that you don't have time for. You have to let friends and family care for you.

Wishing adversity away is only going to make you feel worse about it. Don't fix your eyes on the problem and obsess over it. Instead, hand it over to God and let your heart be soft and open, ready for whatever lessons the School of Patience has for you. Surrender your fear and worry again and again, if necessary. Turn your eyes to the eternal God and watch to see what He does with the situation, with your hand tucked firmly into Jesus' hand.

WORKBOOK

Chapter Three Questions

Question: Think of the difficult things you've gone through in your life. Can you look back on those times and see how they've enabled you to be more empathetic toward others? How have your trials helped you relate to others in a more compassionate manner?

_____

_____

_____

_____

_____

_____

_____

_____

_____

Question: Think of the kinds of things you have done and said to your friends when they were going through challenging circumstances. Based on what you read in this chapter, do you think you were a helpful, empathetic friend, or more like Job's friends? How can you take those experiences and be a better friend moving forward?

_____

_____

_____

_____

_____

_____

_____

_____

_____

Question: Consider the fact that Jesus was without sin, yet He suffered a greater suffering than anyone can fathom. How does that change your perspective on the cause and purpose of suffering? How does it encourage you in your own experiences with suffering?

_____

_____

_____

_____

_____

_____

_____

_____

_____

_____

Action: Do you know anyone who is going through a hard time? Have you been a good friend to that person? Look at the action point titled, "Encourage a Friend," under the Application section in this chapter. Use that section as a guide to reach out to and encourage a friend.

Chapter Three Notes

CHAPTER FOUR

Eternal Perspective

If you're going to wear glasses, it's important to have the right lenses. The world looks fuzzy if your prescription is off. If you have the money, you can get upgraded lenses that promise crisper, more accurate vision.

Have you ever watched a 3D movie without the 3D glasses? It's not particularly magical, is it? Everyone else is gasping and ducking from the illusion of objects flying off the screen, but you just see a flat, fuzzy picture.

In life, we need the right lenses for different circumstances. Sunglasses are useless at night. A pair of 3D glasses serves no purpose outside of the movie theater. A bird watcher is devastated when he forgets his binoculars at home and hears the call of a rare species. For the microbiologist, a microscope must be able to show the tiniest details.

When it comes to our lives, we need the right spiritual lenses, too. Human beings most often live with what I call "temporary lenses" firmly in place. Our attention is fixed on the short span of our lives here on earth.

However, God uses "eternal lenses." His plan isn't limited to making the sixty, seventy, eighty, or so years of your life here on earth as comfortable as possible. Instead, He is preparing us for eternity with Him in heaven.

This is one of the reasons why we struggle so much with our hardships: we're looking at them through our temporary lenses. Learning to use our eternal lenses is an important lesson that is taught in the School of Patience.

Why God Allows Trials

Kids don't see the big picture, do they? As a dad, I understand the consequences of my children forgetting to wear a bike helmet, jumping off the roof, eating their vegetables, and going to bed rather than staying up to watch TV all night. I know that more life is coming, and my children need to be strong and healthy in order to get through. When my four-year-old daughter throws a tantrum because I won't let her have another cookie, she's only looking at this moment. On the other hand, I am taking into account the two cookies she already had and the nutritious dinner I want her to eat in an hour.

I'm convinced that one of the reasons God allows us to go through trials, temptations, and adversity is to reshape and retool the way we view the world and the way we view Him. He sees the eternal consequences of every decision I make, while I can only see a little way down the road. Through the School of Patience, though, it's possible for us to switch our temporary lenses for our eternal ones.

In chapter 21, Job was struggling with his temporary

lenses. He complained through the first part of the chapter that the wicked people of the world seemed to prosper. In Job 21:28–30, he said, "For ye say, Where is the house of the prince? and where are the dwelling places of the wicked? Have ye not asked them that go by the way? and do ye not know their tokens, That the wicked is reserved to the day of destruction? they shall be brought forth to the day of wrath."

I don't know about you, but I've struggled with these same questions. Why do God's people suffer so, when evil people flourish? If all we look at is what we see happening on earth, it can seem really unfair. But once we put on our eternal lenses, we can start to understand that there is something coming for the wicked that will outweigh any suffering we might experience.

Common Belief: Good Reaps Good, Bad Reaps Bad

If you plant apple seeds, an apple tree will grow, right? If you plant poison ivy, you get poison ivy. It's very simple. And this tends to be our expectation of God: I'm doing good things, so I should get good things in return. Never mind that we have a Savior who was perfect and suffered cruelly on earth, reaping a lot of pain for all the "good seeds" He planted.

We keep going back to that Christian "points system." I read my Bible today, so I deserve a few more points in my righteousness bank. Then, I can trade in my "good behavior" points for wealth, health, advancement in my career, and a loving family. I'm sorry to say, there are preachers out there who will tell you that God's plan for your life is for you to be rich and happy all the time.

Romans 2:6–9a tells us:

> *Who will render to every man according to his deeds: to them who by patient continuance and well doing seek for glory and honour and immortality, eternal life: but unto them that are contentious, and do not obey the truth, but obey unrighteousness, indignation and wrath, tribulation and anguish, upon every soul of man that doeth evil....*

We have this idea, and rightfully so, that God is a God who rewards good behavior and punishes bad behavior. However, we start getting off in our theology when we begin to interpret prosperity as indicative of righteousness. Similarly, we are wrong when we view a lack of prosperity as a sign that someone is sinning.

In John 9, Jesus and His disciples came across a blind man. The disciples asked who had sinned to cause his blindness: this man or his parents. Though we might chuckle over this question, the truth is that we do the same thing. And so did Job's friends. They felt the need to have an intervention of sorts with Job, asking him what terrible sin problems he had in his life to cause God's punishment.

I can't help but wonder if this idea of sin causing trouble, and righteousness causing prosperity, isn't just a way of us pretending that we can control what happens in our lives. It's as though we think that if we toe the line, God will notice and reward us. No wonder we are so thrown off balance when we are doing everything "right" and hardship still comes our way! If we see adversity as God's justice for wrongdoing, we will tend to see Him as unjust and unfair.

Judgment Day Is Coming

On the other hand, if you are someone who is indulging in sin, yet things *are* going your way, you might convince yourself that you're getting away with something. Those who suffer abuse might think that their abusers have escaped God's judgment. When we see terrible leaders in other countries who live luxuriously while their people starve, it's tempting to decide that God is permissive.

I'm here to tell you that this is far from the truth. There will be a price to pay. All sin will be accounted for, either through Jesus' work on the cross or in hell for all eternity.

It's time to put on our eternal lenses. Our lives here on earth are a dot on the line of eternity, but what happens here decides what will happen to us for the rest of time. Even a lifetime of suffering now pales in comparison with thousands upon thousands upon thousands of years in heaven in perfect fellowship with God.

For our light affliction, which is but for a moment, worketh for us a far more exceeding and eternal weight of glory; while we look not at the things which are seen, but at the things which are not seen: for the things which are seen are temporal; but the things which are not seen are eternal.

—2 Corinthians 4:17–18

But if we only wear our temporary lenses, all we can see is this small span of years. The School of Patience teaches us to switch to our eternal lenses. We can see our painful circumstances as finite: "Yes, I am in a season of life that is very difficult, but I have an eternity ahead in which I won't even remember this suffering."

It would be nice to be rich, healthy, and happy all the time. However, God has something better in mind for those who love Him. God's purpose for your life isn't temporary comfort; it's eternal fellowship with Him. The two don't even compare!

Whenever my car breaks down, my immediate response, I'm sorry to say, is to complain that this shouldn't happen to me because I tithe. Because I give God ten percent of my income, I expect to receive financial blessing in return, as though tithing were some form of spiritual insurance.

Instead, the School of Patience teaches us that God's blessings come in many forms. Spiritual growth through adversity is one of them. The virtue of empathy is another. Learning to trust in God to provide for us is one of my favorites. We don't know what God's reward for our obedience will be. It might not come to fruition on this earth. I think it's possible that we will earn our rewards in heaven, in many cases.

Unless we are able to take off our temporary lenses, we are never going to be able to see God as just and fair. We must look at eternity. We must trust that God sees things we do not. Like any good father, He sometimes has to say, "Because I know what is best."

Application

1. Ask How This Trial Might Benefit Your Eternity

I don't mean that you should come up with some trite answer. Don't blow this off with, "God must have some purpose that benefits you or Him." Instead, really ask yourself how this trial might benefit eternity. Put some serious thought into it. Jot some notes in your journal or the back of your Bible, where you can reread them periodically.

Consider that these circumstances have an eternal purpose that will far outweigh the present difficulty. Let yourself embrace adversity by putting on your eternal lenses.

2. Don't Envy Those Who Don't Know the Lord

When you check the news and get frustrated because wicked or foolish people are prospering financially or seem to be getting away with something, remember eternity. Psalm 92:7 says, "When the wicked spring as the grass, and when all the workers of iniquity do flourish; it is that they shall be destroyed forever."

Pray against injustice, yes. Ask God to stop abuse of power. Fight against wrongdoing with everything you have. But at the end of the day, know that no sin will go unaccounted for. And we should never throw in the towel and switch sides because we think they're getting rewarded for their crimes.

3. Place Greater Value on Eternity

*But lay up for yourselves treasures in heaven, where nei-
ther moth nor rust doth corrupt, and where thieves do not
break through nor steal: for where your treasure is, there
will your heart be also.*
—Matthew 6:20–21

Wouldn't it be awful to spend so much of our time on earth gathering treasure here that when we get to heaven to spend eternity, we have nothing there?

We must invest in eternal things. Spend time in the Word of God and in prayer. Prioritize church for yourself and your family. See the people around you as your mission field and love them well. Serve others over yourself. Build a relationship with God and be obedient to Him alone.

Because, as we've learned from Job, suffering will happen in our lives. All of the temporary things in which we've invested our time, energy, and money can be gone in a moment. However, our faith in God and our love of our neighbors can't be taken from us. Those are the things that matter most, and the School of Patience has a way of teaching us that the temporary is a house of straw compared to eternity's house of bricks.

WORKBOOK

Chapter Four Questions

Question: Is your perspective of your life characterized more by "temporary lenses" or "eternal lenses"? What changes do you need to make to intentionally maintain an eternally minded perspective?

_____

_____

_____

_____

_____

_____

_____

_____

_____

Question: Do you have the perspective that if you do good, you should receive good from God? How has this false perspective affected your view of God's nature? How do you need to let the Holy Spirit reshape your view on suffering and the nature of God?

_____

_____

_____

_____

_____

_____

_____

_____

_____

_____

Question: When you think about what it would look like for God to bless you, what types of things come to mind? Does what comes to mind reveal a temporary mindset or an eternal one? What are some ways God may want to bless you that have nothing to do with material or physical gain?

_____

_____

_____

_____

_____

_____

_____

_____

_____

_____

_____

Action: Grab a notebook or journal and create two columns. Title one column "Temporary" and the other column "Eternal." As you go throughout your day, filter your activities (and your mindset in those activities) into each column. Use this as an exercise to bring awareness to the motive and focus behind the actions you do. Allow God to show you if your heart is more focused on the temporary or on the eternal. If you need a perspective shift, ask the Holy Spirit to give you an eternal perspective so that you can do all things with eternity in mind.

Chapter Four Notes

CHAPTER FIVE

Faith Without Sight

In C. S. Lewis's book *Mere Christianity*, the author prefaces a chapter on faith by warning that for most people, the content wouldn't apply.[4] Instead, he urges readers to tuck this knowledge away until a time when they would need it.

That's how I want you to look at this chapter. Most readers are not in the middle of a very dark season of life. However, many of you will be there at some point in the future. I want you to have the necessary information now so that you will be ready should you find yourself feeling lost in darkness someday down the road.

Let me begin by talking about the sort of darkness that I mean. I'm not talking about the time when you've been living in rebellion against God and suddenly find yourself dealing with the consequences of your sin. That is a totally different situation.

I'm talking about when you come through so much loss and pain that you are at a crossroads. On one path, you remain trusting in God; the other path leads to giving up on your faith. That is a dark place to be. When a person gets to the point where he or she is questioning God's goodness, even God's existence, it is a lonely, frightening time of life.

As we go through hard seasons, we can hold on to faith for a while. We can keep reminding ourselves that God will provide, that He loves us, and that things will work out for our good. But eventually we grow weary. Our strength comes to an end. And when our fingers start slipping off of our faith, we come to new ground we've never walked before. How do we navigate this dark, lonely place?

Exercising Patience

In Job 22:3–9 and 22:20–29, we see that Eliphaz is talking again. Now he really pulls out all the stops, raking Job over the coals. He accuses Job of being self-righteous, wicked, unkind, guilty, sinful, and proud.

Job answered, "Therefore am I troubled at his presence: when I consider, I am afraid of him. For God maketh my heart soft, and the Almighty troubleth me: because I was not cut off before the darkness, neither hath he covered the darkness from my face" (Job 23:15–17). It was as if Job had been dropped off in the middle of a labyrinth and told to find his way out in complete darkness.

He couldn't understand why God was allowing all of this suffering in his life. And without knowing how to fix the problem, he couldn't find his way through. Repeatedly, Job lamented that if only God would hear his plea, this suffering would come to an end. Job truly believed

God was wrongfully punishing him. And if his suffering wasn't a punishment, Job longed to know what the real cause was.

I think that gets to the bottom of the issue with which many of us struggle: we believe we could more cheerfully face adversity if only we understood the end game. We're okay with suffering if we know that it serves a purpose. We're willing to go to the gym and endure a grueling workout because we know that the results are weight loss and building muscle. Sacrificing time and money so we can get another college degree works out in the end when we get a promotion and a raise.

Going through suffering makes us feel like we are on one side of a great chasm and God is on the other. As our suffering continues, we might eventually feel that we are on one side and everyone we love is on the other side. It's easy to believe that *understanding the purpose of it all* would be the bridge that gets us back across.

But that isn't how God does things. It might seem obvious, but one of the virtues we gain from the School of Patience is exercising patience. You see, we don't just want to understand the purpose of our hardships in order to get closer to God. We want to understand what is going on so that we can fix it! Then we don't have to wait on God anymore. We can just solve everything ourselves.

Job believed that if only he could understand God's reasons for his suffering, it would make his pain more tolerable. He wanted light in his labyrinth of pain, thinking it would help him get out of the maze more quickly.

God Has GPS

Despite Job's desperate desire for understanding, God denied him. Job wasn't given an explanation. God kept him in the dark. If you are in similar, dark circumstances, know that you might not get the illumination you believe you need in order to get through. Still, you haven't been abandoned by God.

A few years back, when our kids were still little, we went to a corn maze with a group of friends. It was fall, which meant it got dark early and the temperatures could really plunge when the sun went down. It wasn't my first time going to this particular farm. However, every year, the maze had a different design. Thinking that I'd done this before and feeling pretty cocky, I jumped right in, leading the way.

But time kept ticking by, and we remained lost in the maze. It was getting cold. The kids were getting hungry. That's when I realized I had no idea how to get out of the maze. And do you want to know the worst of it? I had a map the whole time.

I kid you not. I had a map and *still* couldn't get us out. The problem was that I had no idea where we were on that map. I could see the entrance and the exit, but I couldn't figure out where exactly we were in relation to those two places.

That describes how we feel when we are in the midst of adversity, doesn't it? Afterward, we can look back and remember how we got into the maze. We know exactly what it will look and feel like to get out of the maze. But it's the part in the middle that is disorienting. You could be two turns away from the exit or still stuck near the entrance. Any turn you make could be the wrong one, taking you farther from the desired escape.

So, what are we to do?

When you are in the midst of difficult circumstances and can't see what to do—when you don't know where to go—it's time to stop trying to lead the way. Stop squinting ahead or behind, trying to make out shapes in the dark.

Instead, surrender to God. Put your hand firmly in His and let Him lead. When we do not know what to do, we need to put our trust in the one who knows exactly where we are and how to get to the exit. God is never lost. He's right there in the maze, in the dark, with us, except He has night vision goggles and GPS. Job said it in chapter 23, verse 10: "But [God] knoweth the way that I take: when he hath tried me, I shall come forth as gold."

It's vital for us to understand that God is working the whole time we are suffering. Not only is He standing next to us and offering comfort, but He's also clearing away obstacles that are coming up ahead of us. You might have to stand still longer than you like, because God is busy working on something you can't see. He's bringing things together, just out of sight—but because we can't see it, we assume He's forgotten about us.

Remember that you are not alone in the darkness. You might not be able to see through the dark, but God can. You just need to trust Him to walk you through it. In fact, I believe that is exactly what He is forcing you to do. He is preventing you from the fleshly habit of walking by sight, forcing you to walk by faith instead. Refusing to let you lean on your own understanding, He is backing you up against a Red Sea, where you have to trust Him with all your heart.

Heart Softener

Not only did Job take comfort in God's knowledge of him, but he took comfort in the process. Read Job 23:10 again. Do you see what Job was doing there? He recognized that there was a good process taking place. He didn't understand it, nor did he necessarily like it, but he trusted that something good was happening.

Job knew God was refining and purifying him. God was sifting his beliefs to expose the wrong ones. The things Job was depending on for comfort and provision were removed. God stripped those things away and left only Himself.

In Job 23:16, Job said, "God maketh my heart soft." This idea of having a soft heart is familiar to us Christians. When Jesus gave the parable of the seeds being scattered, He told us that only those people who offer good soil would be able to accept the seeds and grow strong plants (Matthew 13:1–9, 18–23). The good soil represents a soft heart, willing and ready to hear what the Holy Spirit has to say.

Have you ever gone through a troubling time and found fresh comfort in God's Word? Suddenly, the Psalms mean more to you, the Gospels offer such promise, and maybe even the book of Job soothes your soul. The School of Patience has a way of softening us and opening us up so that we can absorb spiritual things better. Once we surrender the need to shove our way through to the solution, and start letting God lead us, we become much more willing to hear His voice.

It's like what they say about a person who loses his or her sight: the other senses become more noticeable. We depend so heavily on our eyesight that we don't give our hearing and sense of smell as much attention. Once sight is gone, our brains can notice what our other senses have been telling us all along.

When we can no longer trust our own judgment, we are forced to trust God's. This opens up our ability, our willingness, to be led in other areas. Our hearts are made soft.

Application

1. Trust God with Your Darkness

It's counterintuitive. We are modern Americans, after all! When life knocks us down, we pull ourselves up by our bootstraps and press on. We like the idea of being "self-made."

Yet, when we find ourselves lost in the dark, our first reaction should be to stop trying to lead and begin relinquishing control to God. We need to stop trying to fix our darkness. Instead, we must trust that God has a good purpose for it. We need to wait patiently for Him to lead us through to the light.

Let me offer you this warning, from a place of humility and compassion: not understanding why you are suffering is no reason to take a vacation from reading your Bible and praying. In fact, the opposite is true. When adversity hits, we should run right to our Bibles and draw comfort in pouring out our hearts to God in prayer.

2. Stop Trying to Figure It All Out

Trusting God is more important than having the right answers. I am a figure-it-out-er. I like strategizing and coming up with workable solutions. I don't necessarily think that's a bad thing. However, surrendering to God is a lesson I have had to learn in the School of Patience. Seasons of suffering can't be navigated by my analytical prowess. I have to let God lead while I remain in the dark.

In Philippians 4:6–7, Paul admonished:

> *Be careful for nothing; but in every thing by prayer and supplication with thanksgiving let your requests be made known unto God. And the peace of God, which passeth all understanding, shall keep your hearts and minds through Christ Jesus.*

God's antidote to worry and anxiety is not problem-solving but trusting Christ with the problem. Though you cannot see God or what He is doing, He knows exactly where you are, and He knows how to get you to the exit.

3. Trust in the Refining Process

I can't tell you why, exactly, God allows suffering into your life. I can give you general reasons, but not specific ones. Still, knowing the general purposes God has for adversity can help to make it more bearable.

God is working tremendously in your life. If you let Him lead you through the darkness, you will come out on the other side in far better shape, spiritually. Suffering has a way of stripping away the unnecessary things from our lives. It whittles away our idols. It reveals sinful thought processes and habits. You are growing stronger with every trusting step you take. You are gaining new tools and greater wisdom all the time.

Let this knowledge fuel your drive not to lose your grip on your faith in God.

Chapter Five Questions

Question: *We're okay with suffering if we know that it serves a purpose.* Have you ever found yourself bargaining with God, "If You would only show me *why* I am going through this, I could endure it a little longer." Why do you think it's important to trust God even when—especially when—you don't know or understand why you are going through suffering?

_____

_____

_____

_____

_____

_____

_____

_____

_____

_____

_____

Question: In this difficult time of your life, are you still trying to "solve" your way out of it? Are you still blindly charging ahead to find your own solutions? Have you taken the time to truly relinquish control and trust God's guidance? If not, confess this to God and ask Him to bring you back to a place of surrender and trust.

_____

_____

_____

_____

_____

_____

_____

_____

_____

_____

_____

Question: _I had a map the whole time._ God has provided you with His Word, prayer, and worship as guiding lights through your dark days. During this trial, have you had the tendency to run into God's Word and presence, or away from them? If you find yourself putting more distance between you and the things of God, you need to course correct. Make some time and space every day to spend time with God as you go through this difficult season.

_____

_____

_____

_____

_____

_____

_____

_____

_____

_____

_____

Action: Find an image of a person standing at a crossroads. On one road write, "Continue trusting in God." On the other road, write, "Walk away from my faith." On the back of the picture, create a list of all the personal and biblical reasons you have for continuing to trust in God. You may not be standing at such a crossroads right now, but someday you may be faced with that decision. Keep this picture in a safe place for that day. And when you find yourself at a crossroads, take out the photo and review your list of why you should continue trusting in God.

Chapter Five Notes

Part Two:
Knowing God
Through Suffering

CHAPTER SIX

The Nature of Godly Wisdom

In 1984, the movie *The Karate Kid* was released.[5] In it, a high school boy by the name of Daniel moves to a new town in California. He comes up against a group of bullies who are all training in karate. Luckily for Daniel, his neighbor, Mr. Miyagi, just happens to be a karate whiz and is willing to teach Daniel what he knows.

Now, Mr. Miyagi's training is strange. He requires his pupil to wash Mr. Miyagi's windows, wax his car, practice crane kicks on a post on the beach, catch a fly with chopsticks, and perform his moves while balancing in a boat. At first, Daniel questions this training and even gets angry with Mr. Miyagi. But once the older man demonstrates that these things are teaching Daniel's muscles the right moves for karate, he changes his tune.

Of course, that doesn't mean Daniel would be excited about waxing anyone else's car. If a stranger came up and told him to get in a boat and start practicing blocks, Daniel would think the guy was nuts. If his mom asked him to sand the floor or paint the fence, he probably would moan and groan, knowing these were simply chores and not karate training.

You see, Daniel comes to understand that Mr. Miyagi's training regimen is unusual but effective. He trusts his teacher and knows his voice. In the middle of his big fight against the bullies, Daniel can hear Mr. Miyagi calling from the crowd and follows his instructions.

The past five chapters of this book have focused on virtues we learn in the School of Patience: having a proper paradigm for problems, Christ-centered faith, empathy, eternal perspective, and faith without sight. Now, I want to shift to something else we must learn.

You see, we're never going to get far if we don't know our Creator well. Unless we understand some fundamental truths about Him, we're doomed to fail. When we are in that dark place, feeling alone and lost, without knowing what is true, our emotions are going to tell us a different story. *Along with virtues, the School of Patience imparts a deeper knowledge of who God is.*

In this chapter, I want to focus on God's wisdom. The Bible tells us repeatedly that God is wise. Still, there are times when we face a decision and don't know which way to go. This is when we need to understand the nature of God's wisdom and be able to identify His voice.

Elihu

Remember how Job had three friends sitting and arguing with him? So far, we've heard plenty from Eliphaz and Bildad, and Zophar chimed in, too (in Job 11 and 20). But then came Elihu. Once Job had gone back and forth with the first three friends, Elihu finally jumped in (Job 32). Unlike the other three, Elihu waited to speak. He listened to Job defend himself and lament God's actions. And while Elihu didn't get everything right, he did make a few points that I think are spot on.

It's worth noting that Elihu was the only one of the five men in the book of Job who didn't get corrected by God. God reprimanded Eliphaz, Zophar, and Bildad, and Job himself, but not Elihu. I think this is one way we know that Elihu was speaking with godly wisdom. Similarly, Job didn't have an answer for Elihu. Even though Elihu gave Job time to answer him, Job stayed silent.

So, despite the fact that Elihu was the youngest, he was also a man with a good deal of godly wisdom. Job would have done well to listen to this friend. The point here is not to specify the advice given by Elihu. Rather, it is to teach us what good advice looks like and sounds like so that we might better listen to it when it comes around.

Godly Wisdom Versus Worldly Wisdom

It's so important for us to be able to recognize people who are speaking godly wisdom in our lives. Eliphaz and Bildad had a lot to say, but their so-called wisdom was based in their worldly perceptions. Rather than uplift Job, their words dragged him down.

If you've ever spent much time reading the book of Proverbs, you've noticed the theme of trusting godly wisdom over worldly wisdom. Things that make sense to us when we have our temporary lenses in place are absolutely ridiculous when we put on our eternal lenses.

James 3:17 tells us, "But the wisdom that is from above is first pure, then peaceable, gentle, and easy to be intreated, full of mercy and good fruits, without partiality, and without hypocrisy."

There are always going to be a bevy of voices calling out and trying to tell you what to do. It's not as simple as good and pure loved ones saying one thing while cackling bad guys twirl their mustaches and call out bad advice. Even friends and family members we trust can pull out their worldly wisdom from time to time, and it's up to us to know the difference.

We must take time to get familiar with God's wisdom. That starts with studying the Bible. God's wisdom is woven throughout Scripture; it's in every book from start to finish. When we read the Bible, we begin to build an understanding of who God is and what His character is. When we face situations in our lives, we know inherently whether or not God would approve of certain decisions.

The second thing we must do is spend time in prayer. We must ask God to direct our steps and help us to know when to move forward and when to stay still. In short, we need to be able to recognize the Holy Spirit's promptings. Then, when we face a difficult decision, no matter what anyone around us says, we have the ability to sift out the worldly advice and hold on to the godly advice.

1. Godly Wisdom Is Humble

One thing we can always know about godly wisdom is that it is humble. Elihu demonstrated that for us. He waited and listened, recognizing that his youth put him at a disadvantage in the argument. Meekly, he allowed the others to go first, believing that their words would be wiser than his own. This is in keeping with Proverbs 15:28, which says, "The heart of the righteous studyeth to answer, but the mouth of the wicked poureth out evil things."

Be careful when you have someone who's always quick with the answers. Do you know someone like that? Whenever you talk about what's happening, this person jumps in first and tells you exactly what you should do. Now, could this person have godly wisdom? Yes, of course. But that need to jump in and tell you what to do isn't in keeping with biblical humility. Regardless, hold up this person's advice against what you know of God and what the Holy Spirit is telling you—don't just grab the advice and run.

2. Godly Wisdom Is Based in Truth

Once there were three sisters. One of them began to show signs of dementia when she was in her fifties. Her loving husband, Bob, patiently cared for her for ten years before finally admitting that her needs were more than he could handle. He then found a wonderful care facility for his wife.

However, Bob had also been growing close to a woman from his church. As his wife had slipped further and further from him, Bob found himself falling in love with this other woman. Worried that his sisters-in-law might condemn him if he made a move, Bob reached out to them and asked their advice.

Though both women professed to be Christians, they had very different answers. The first sister wrote back quickly, telling Bob that he had "paid his dues" with his wife and deserved to enjoy life. She supported his decision to begin a relationship with this other woman even though his wife was still alive.

The second sister did not agree. Even though her heart went out to Bob, she could not approve of this relationship. The Bible was very clear that marriage is to be until death. So long as Bob was married, it would be sinful to date anyone else, no matter the circumstances. With a heavy heart, the second sister told this to Bob. It wasn't what Bob wanted to hear, and he grew very angry.

The voice of wisdom is passionate about the truth. Elihu got upset with Job and the other men because they'd been giving faulty advice. Their accusations and Job's rebuttal weren't taking into account the truth of God's identity.

The wisdom of God will have a fierce devotion to God's truth above all else. That is how you can know it is trustworthy and believable. Truth is the North Star that allows us to make sure we are plotting the right course in life. Godly wisdom will never contradict what is stated in the Bible.

3. Godly Wisdom Is Impartial

Godly wisdom isn't biased. It doesn't change or make exceptions. No matter what the circumstances, godly wisdom holds us all to the same standard. It doesn't change based on the audience, the culture of the time, or fear of hurting feelings.

Now, that doesn't mean we can use godly wisdom as a steamroller to crush everyone in our path. In fact, godly wisdom gives us the ability to discern when to speak and when to be silent; when to speak gently and when to speak firmly. We might have a friend who wants us to be a straight shooter and get to the point. Another friend might need us to ask probing questions, helping him to realize the truth for himself or herself.

It's tempting to be more concerned with backing up our friends than helping them find the truth, isn't it? A guy you know says, "Man, my wife is driving me crazy," and we men have a knee-jerk response of, "Women are like that." A woman says, "I hate my boss. I want to quit my job." As a friend, it's easy to respond with, "Just do it. Find a job that makes you happy!"

But are these answers based in godly wisdom? Would we reply the same way to our children, to our parents, or to other friends? If not, it's a good sign that we are being biased and, therefore, not being led by God's wisdom.

Godly wisdom must be the same for this person as it is for that person. It is the same no matter what. It cannot be adjusted. God's wisdom needs to be objective and unbiased. How we deliver it can change, but the truth cannot.

Learning to Distinguish God's Voice

Proverbs 3:5–6 says, "Trust in the LORD with all thine heart; and lean not unto thine own understanding." Sometimes, the temptation to rely on our own understanding gets the better of us—but when this happens, we so often regret it later. We realize belatedly that we made a decision or a move because we thought it made sense, not because of the Holy Spirit's promptings.

We have a family friend whose son is a golf pro. He has told me before that one of the hardest things he does is helping his clients unlearn bad habits. I think we Christians have a lot of bad habits when it comes to decision making, particularly in painful seasons of our lives. The urge to get ourselves away from the hurt overrides our ability to listen for God and make wise decisions.

The School of Patience wants us to learn how to distinguish God's wisdom. For one thing, this wisdom is what helps us to navigate seasons of adversity without panic. Instead, we can recognize that God has lessons for us to learn, and we can trust Him to get us through.

So, how do we learn to recognize godly wisdom? Again, we do it through getting to know God. Habits like reading our Bibles, spending time both talking and listening in prayer, and finding good teachers will all help.

We must stop being enamored of our own wisdom. It's as James said: "But let him ask in faith, nothing wavering. For he that wavereth is like a wave of the sea driven with the wind and tossed" (James 1:6). Just like Daniel has to learn to do things Mr. Miyagi's way in order to keep from falling off his post during his crane kicks, we have to learn to do things God's way.

Application

1. Listen to the Wisdom That Is Humble

You're going through some of the hardest things you've ever had to endure. A dear family member calls you up and asks you to meet him for lunch. You sit in the restaurant and lay out your situation. This beloved person opens his mouth and starts talking. He brags about his knowledge of the world, his success in business, and how well he's come through the few problems he's ever faced.

An earmark of godly wisdom is humility. Though there might be some good advice in this man's speech, it needs to be considered carefully. In fact, if you knew in advance that this person was so proud, it would have been wiser not to entrust your pain to him, no matter how much love you bear toward each other.

2. Listen to the Wisdom That Is Biblical

We must make sure that wisdom is straight and true— that it lines up with the Bible. Again and again, it's vital to pull out the Word of God and check that we are going in the right direction.

Don't fall into the trap of ceasing to study Scripture when trouble hits. When you're outside of those especially difficult periods of life, it's easy to wonder why anyone who's suffering would forget to read the Bible. But when a loved one falls ill, a job is lost, or a marriage crumbles, it's hard to remain faithful in our study of the Word.

Without it, though, we will not be able to recognize godly wisdom when it comes. We'll be led more easily into the dead-end tunnels of our labyrinth.

3. Listen to the Wisdom That Is Impartial

As hard as it might be, godly wisdom shouldn't pull any punches. It should hit us square in the heart every time. And, if we're honest, we know when we're being given advice that is only what we want to hear. Godly wisdom cuts through all of the nonsense and is fresh and life-giving.

Don't let yourself fail to say what is true to friends who are hurting. Commiserating only allows the wound to fester. Unbiased truth spoken with love washes away the cloudy residue that obscures our vision.

WORKBOOK

Chapter Six Questions

Question: Describe what you believe godly wisdom is. How does it compare and contrast with worldly wisdom? In your trials, have you been paying more attention to worldly wisdom or to godly wisdom?

_____

_____

_____

_____

_____

_____

_____

_____

_____

_____

Question: Think about the conversations you've had with friends and mentors about your difficult situation. Evaluate the responses from each encounter. Which responses have been rooted in worldly wisdom? Which have been rooted in godly wisdom? Which advice are you more inclined to lean into? How does thinking about it in terms of worldly versus godly wisdom affect how you will respond to their advice?

_____

_____

_____

_____

_____

_____

_____

_____

_____

_____

Question: Think about the advice you've received from friends and mentors that has most stood out to you—the advice that you have grabbed hold of, to walk you through this time. Write out this advice that most stuck with you. Now evaluate it. Is the advice humble? Is it rooted in God's Word? Is it without partiality? Based on this assessment, is it still advice worth holding on to?

_____

_____

_____

_____

_____

_____

_____

_____

_____

_____

_____

Action: Read and memorize Proverbs 3:5–6: "Trust in the LORD with all thine heart; and lean not unto thine own understanding. In all thy ways acknowledge him, and he shall direct thy paths." As you walk through your suffering, seeking answers and guidance, filter your feedback through those verses. Commit before God to lean on His understanding rather than give in to the answers that merely feel comfortable. In a journal or notebook, write the different ways you have been tempted to lean on your own understanding. Then, for each point, write a response that is rooted in godly wisdom.

Chapter Six Notes

CHAPTER SEVEN

Knowing the Creator

A man—we'll call him Tony—is on trial, never mind what for. He's been accused of a crime, and the lawyers are doing battle. After preparing for months, they now lay out their arguments. The prosecuting attorney brings witnesses to prove that Tony is guilty. She enters into evidence his phone records, his banking statements, and a highly incriminating text message. Tony gets worried.

But then it's the defense lawyer's turn. He gets up and refutes what the other lawyer said. Now Tony's mom, his boss, and a friend from church get a chance to say what a great guy he is. For every piece of evidence the prosecutor produced, the defense attorney has a reply.

After all of the back-and-forth arguments between the prosecution and defense, at the end of the day, it is all up to the judge. Regardless of what either side argues, what the judge has to say is all that eventually counts.

In chapter 38 of the book of Job, God has heard enough. He heard Eliphaz's accusations and Bildad's arguments. He heard Job's wails of despair. He even heard

Elihu stand up for Him. Now it was time for the Judge to speak. And when *He* spoke, it wasn't mere opinion, but pure truth.

He did not disappoint: "Then, the LORD answered Job out of the whirlwind, and said, Who is this that darkeneth council by words without knowledge? Gird up now thy loins like a man; for I will demand of thee, and answer thou me'" (Job 38:1–3).

I don't know about you, but I sure wouldn't want to be in Job's shoes! It's one thing to quietly grumble that God isn't on your side. It's a whole other thing to have Him arrive via cyclone to tell you you're in the wrong.

Dark Counsel

That phrase "darkeneth council" resonates with me. Council is supposed to enlighten us—to show us the right way to go. To darken council is to give bad advice or to say things that are inaccurate. Any time someone tries to give advice that isn't grounded in God's truth, he's darkening counsel; he's obscuring the truth by his advice. Dark council paints a faulty picture of who God is. It suggests that God is unfair, unjust, and unloving.

Job, Eliphaz, and Bildad were doing this very thing for more than thirty chapters. Eliphaz and Bildad painted a picture of God as unmerciful and exacting. In response, Job's laments suggested that God was ignoring him and punishing him without reason. No wonder God wanted to set them straight!

It's easy for us to criticize these men. The truth is that we face (and, let's be honest, give into) this temptation all the time. Maybe we don't sit for a week in the dirt wailing, but we do plenty of quiet griping. Without having the full picture, we can believe and say all sorts of things about God and our situation that aren't even close to true.

We watch a loved one suffer and start distancing ourselves from God without ever articulating that we are angry with Him for allowing this to happen. When someone tells us about their trouble, we pop off a response that is clearly not in line with the Bible. All of these responses trumpet the fact that our understanding of God and reality is darkened.

God Draws a Clear Picture

But, as we can see in Job 38, God will not tolerate His children painting a distorted picture of Him. Jesus, in John 17:3, said, "And this is life eternal, that they might know thee the only true God, and Jesus Christ, whom thou hast sent." Knowing God in truth is the point of eternity! It isn't just about strolling the golden streets and hanging out with the Apostles.

If God values our intimate knowledge of Him so much, we can see why He isn't going to put up with our dark council. He will correct our false ideas. He will bring discipline into our lives to get us back on track. Knowing God is the ultimate prize. He's going to help His children win it.

This is another way the School of Patience works in our lives. Suffering strips away the things that don't really matter and frequently brings us into closer communion with God. It is in these seasons of deep affliction and close communion that God reveals Himself to us in greater ways.

In Job 38–41, this is exactly what's happening with Job. We might have thought that when He finally spoke, God would explain *why* everything had happened to Job. But there isn't one word that explains the *why*. Instead, God laid out His resumé for Job, letting Himself be known in all His glory.

God created and sustains the universe. He built the foundations of the earth, measuring it out and planning every detail. He keeps the oceans in their place. He knows the storehouse where all the snowflakes are kept. He manages storms. He makes the sun come up and go down. He feeds the lions and waters the jungles. He freezes water. He created the concept of rain and dew.

On and on God talked, declaring His awesome abilities. Remember, Job had a "darkened" view of God—one that was too small and distorted. This is often what suffering reveals about us: we've got a faulty, small view of God. This resumé of God's power was given to fix that. Through difficult times, God wants to reveal that He is bigger and better than you have been imagining Him to be.

Humble Yourself Before the Creator

After hearing such a list, there was nothing for Job to do but humbly accept that he was wrong. In light of all of this, Job could clearly see that he was wrongfully accusing God and needed to repent.

But God also needed to reset Job's perceptions. Trials

have a way of doing just that. The School of Patience puts us through a refining fire, and all the dross is burned away. Our egos get cut down to size. As we fix our eyes on the eternal, we recognize how small we are and how big and good God really is.

Seasons of adversity open up our hearts and reveal many hidden things. Pride, apathy, selfishness, and wrong beliefs about God all come bubbling up to the surface. Think of Peter at the Last Supper when he insisted that he would never abandon Jesus. What did he do the instant things got scary? Peter denied ever knowing Jesus (John 18:13–27).

This is one of the purposes God has for hard times. He gets us to the point where we have to stop our whining, posturing, begging, and raging and face the reality of Him. Then we can do nothing but stand meekly before the one who created the building blocks of the universe and repent.

Does this fix our circumstances instantly? No, it doesn't. Knowing the reality of God isn't the twelfth step of the "make my life prosperous" ladder. It's not a way to manipulate God into doing what we want. After God laid out His resumé to Job, He didn't bring Job's ten children back to life. What He did do was reveal Himself to Job in a way that few others have ever experienced. To put it simply, Job got to know God on a much deeper level through this season of suffering. And knowing God is what eternal life is all about.

A right walk with God through this life isn't marked by the absence of difficulties. It is marked by the ability to endure them gracefully, to wear the scars we've earned along the way with dignity, and to carry with us an un-shakable faith in the God who is infinitely wiser and more competent than we are.

Application

1. Be Careful Not to Trivialize God

I think it's incredibly important to humble ourselves regularly through worship. Taking a cool view of God is dangerous to our faith. If you are too proud to bow your heart before God, you need to spend some time searching your heart and repenting. I know a woman who has set a reminder on her phone to focus on something awesome about God three times a day. Perhaps you could implement a time to "pause and praise" God for one of His awe-inspiring attributes. As we've seen, God won't stand for His children to have a false view of Him. Repent now, or be ready for God to humble you later.

2. Develop a Bigger View of God by Observing Nature

Spending time in nature is one way to reorient our perspective of God. I believe this is one of the fascinating lessons from Job: nature reveals aspects of God and His nature to us. It's difficult to see a towering tree, a beautiful sunrise, or a colorful bird and not marvel at the Creator. Things we hardly ever think about are managed perfectly around us all the time while we are busy with our little lives.

Go for a hike. Ride your bike along a wooded trail.

Take a run where you can see someone's lovely garden. Remember that God invented all these things, manages all these things, and still has time to care for the details of your everyday life.

3. Develop a Bigger View of God Through Worship

Another way to keep God in the right place is through reading your Bible and personal worship. Even if you aren't a great singer or don't connect well through musical worship, it's still possible to marvel at God's glory.

Write a list of ways in which God amazes you. Sit quietly and list His attributes. Imagine yourself walking into a room where He is waiting for you; walk up to Him and tell Him that you love Him. And, yes, sing songs of praise even if you can't carry a tune in a bucket.

WORKBOOK

Chapter Seven Questions

Question: What thoughts about God have come up for you during this time of suffering? Have the responses from friends and mentors reinforced or challenged these ideas about God? Are these ideas in alignment with who God says He is?

_____

_____

_____

_____

_____

_____

_____

_____

_____

Question: Have you made assumptions about God's nature during your suffering? Have you falsely accused God throughout this time? If so, write down those assumptions and false accusations. For each, write the corresponding truth about God, and repent for each wrong assumption you've held because of your suffering.

_____

_____

_____

_____

_____

_____

_____

_____

_____

Question: Is your view of God too "cool"? Do you find it too difficult to humble yourself before Him? Are you resistant to posturing yourself in a place of surrender, humility, and praise? If so, repent for trivializing God, and take steps toward gaining a bigger view of Him, such as spending time in nature and in worship.

_____

_____

_____

_____

_____

_____

_____

_____

_____

_____

Action: Read Job 38–41. Make a list of all of the different attributes of God you can find in those chapters. What do you think God is trying to convey about His character and nature through this monologue? With those characteristics in mind, write a one-page (or shorter) description of who God has revealed Himself to be and who He is to you. When you find yourself confused and questioning God's nature and character, refer to this description.

Chapter Seven Notes

CHAPTER EIGHT

Knowing the Sustainer

Any time you start looking for work, you have to get out your resumé, dust it off, and add whatever new skills you've gained since you last applied for a job. There's a place to list your work experience, your education, and any pertinent skills.

Depending on the job you're applying for, you might add or delete a few things. Your typing speed isn't impressive if you're trying to get a job pouring cement, but it would be helpful if you'd like to work in the front office.

In Job 38–42, God gives us His resumé. It's pretty impressive. But there's something else I want you to notice: God is telling us about the specifics of the role He wants to play in our lives. He is giving us His resumé to tell us why He's trustworthy and capable.

When we find ourselves in painful seasons of life, we might doubt whether God can really be trusted with our lives. Again and again, we're hit with waves of uncertainty. In those times, we need to know that not only is God *able* to care for us, but He is also *actively* caring for us. We need to understand that He is the Sustainer of the Universe.

This resumé is what finally helped Job repent of his wrong beliefs and reorient his thinking about God. For thirty-some chapters in Job, people were talking, but what changed everything was when God stepped in and laid out His resumé. When Job heard God's voice clearly, he surrendered his doubts.

Our Sustainer

If these last chapters of Job are God's resumé, the first "job" on the list would be Creator of the Universe. Job 38 paints a vivid picture of God's awesome ability to create everything we see and, in particular, what we can't see.

The next qualification that God laid out in chapter 39 was Sustainer of the Universe. He did this in a very clever way. God listed nine different animals and explained how He sustains them. By doing this, He showed us a number of important roles He plays in our lives.

I want to highlight five of these roles that demonstrate how God is using the School of Patience to teach us that He is the trustworthy sustainer of our lives.

1. Constant Care Through Lonely Places

Who hath sent out the wild ass free? or who hath loosed the bands of the wild ass? Whose house I have made the wilderness, and the barren land his dwellings. He scorneth the multitude of the city, neither regardeth he the crying of the driver. The range of the mountains is his pasture, and he searcheth after every green thing.

—*Job 39:5–8*

In the first eight verses of this chapter, God referred to wild goats, hyenas, and donkeys. He began by describing how He knew them in the womb and helped them to be birthed. God has been involved in their lives from the start and stays with them through their old age. Though they live in lonely, barren places, God provides for their needs.

The same is true for us. God knew you in the womb. He's cared for you as a child, a teen, and a young adult, and will be with you through your last days. He knows how to care for and develop your life, and the proof is in how He cares for the wild donkeys, hyenas, and goats.

I'm struck by the loneliness of these three animals. They aren't cute, cuddly species who are petted and cooed over. Hyenas are often painted as the bad guys. They might be sociable with each other, but they are scavengers. No one else wants to hang out with the hyenas.

Similarly, donkeys are rarely the heroes of the tale. In fact, they're mostly known for being stubborn.

When I picture wild goats, I imagine rocky, barren mountainsides. The goats have to travel far to find a mouthful of grass to eat. The weather is harsh, and there are few good places to shelter, not to mention plenty of enemies. Wild goats have to be tough.

Unlovable. Stubborn. Tough. When we go through long periods of adversity, those words feel like familiar descriptors. We might be hanging on, but our hands are raw from the harsh elements. Only sheer stubbornness has kept us from giving up. And that isn't a particularly love-able, cuddly frame of mind.

Yet God sustains these animals, and He will sustain you. Though you are in a barren, lonely place, God will not abandon you. It's possible to go through the harshest conditions in life because we know the Sustainer of the Universe. Look how He cares for the hyenas, the wild goats, and the donkeys.

2. Tamer of Wild Hearts

Canst thou bind the unicorn with his band in the furrow? or will he harrow the valleys after thee? Wilt thou trust him, because his strength is great? or wilt thou leave thy labour to him?

—Job 39:10–11

I have to admit, I really like that the King James Version names this animal the unicorn. Personally, I think this might describe a rhinoceros, as it has horns like a unicorn and is impossible to tame.

Either way, the picture that is painted here is fantastic. Can you imagine someone trapping a wild rhinoceros and then fitting it to his plow? It's absurd! The strength of a rhinoceros would be far too much to tame and force to do something as mundane as plowing.

Even if you could tame a rhino, would you trust him not to trample everything? You wouldn't want him in the pen with the cows or the pigs in case he got it in his mind to start tearing everything up.

Yet God created these incredible beasts—and what's

more, He controls them. God can do what we cannot. He can do what we cannot even *imagine* doing. He can tame the wildest of hearts without batting an eye. Imagine what He can do in your life.

When you feel like your life is spinning out of control, remember that God hasn't lost His grip on the reins. It might seem that a rhinoceros has been hitched to the plow of your life, but that doesn't worry the Sustainer of the Universe.

And if you've run away and don't know if you can find your way back, there's good news: God is able to tame the wild rhinoceros, and He can tame your wild heart, too. He can tame the heart of your wild son or daughter or husband or sibling. God is big enough, and He is in control.

3. Beauty and Protection

Gavest thou the goodly wings unto the peacocks? or wings and feathers unto the ostrich? which leaveth her eggs in the earth, and warmeth them in dust....
—Job 39:13–14

Here are two very different birds that demonstrate two interesting aspects of the Sustainer of the Universe. God designed the peacock to be very beautiful. There is purpose in beauty, and it is a good thing. Male birds are often colorful and flashy, so they can distract potential hunters from their mates who are sitting with the eggs. Colorful flowers attract bees to spread their pollen.

Not only is color functional in these ways, but it is also beautiful. God gave us eyes to see colors, and He gave us an appreciation of beauty. When our hearts are heavy, we have the ability to go into nature and find joy in His creation.

But what I find especially interesting is the mention of the ostrich and what God says about it. Here, God points out that the ostrich lays her eggs in the dirt and then abandons them. This seems like an example of bad mothering, doesn't it? Yet it's how God created her to be. Despite this apparent abandonment, ostriches still exist and continue reproducing.

I think this teaches us two lessons. First, the ostrich does what it's designed to do. For whatever reason, ostrich mothers abandon their eggs rather than sit on them. This is part of how God hardwired them. They give birth and don't seem to have the instinct to stick around. Despite their poor maternal instincts and lack of wisdom, ostriches still exist, because God makes it so.

The second lesson we can learn from the ostrich is that when we are foolish of our own accord, God is still able to sustain us. God's ability to sustain your life isn't dependent on your level of understanding. In other words, to survive, you don't have to understand everything that God does.

Even when we make a major error in judgment, God is able to sustain us. We don't have to possess all the right answers; only God does. Think about this in terms of your children. They don't have great wisdom and understanding, yet you take care of them, just as God cares for you. Your son might make a huge mistake, but you don't stop loving and caring for him. Instead, you help him set things right and keep providing for him.

God is going to work something beautiful in your life. Look at how He designed the peacock and how He keeps the ostriches alive. You matter far more than either the peacock or the ostrich. God will sustain you.

4. The Gift of Strength

Hast thou given the horse strength? hast thou clothed his neck with thunder? canst thou make him afraid as a grasshopper? the glory of his nostrils is terrible.
—Job 39:19–20

Consider the horse. He is strong and courageous. Horses take riders into battle without fear. I love the language that God uses in verse 24: "[The horse] swallowth the ground with fierceness and rage: neither believeth he that it is the sound of the trumpet." The trumpets, shouting, and banging of swords on shields don't frighten the horse one little bit.

God designed some animals to have strength and courage. They are gifts from the Creator. Though you might be in a dark place and feel anything but strong or brave, know that God is able to gift you with these virtues. You might be at the end of your ability to fight, but the God who made horses strong isn't done with you yet. He has endless resources to pour out on you.

5. Soar to High Places

Doth the hawk fly by thy wisdom, and stretch her wings toward the south? Doth the eagle mount up at thy command, and make her nest on high?
—Job 39:26–27

Consider the birds of prey. Eons before the Wright brothers got their first plane off the ground, birds were soaring through the air. In fact, the early pioneers of flight studied birds in order to figure out how to build the first airplanes. They needed God's blueprints in order to build a replica.

And though flight has come a long way, we still don't have the bird's natural skill. We can't flap our wings and rise to great heights, hover on a strong breeze, turn on a dime, or nest in a high crag. Yet God created these huge birds to do these very things, and He did so apart from the aid of our understanding.

I believe a major theme in this section of Scripture is that there are many things God does beyond our understanding or power; but they are still awesome, beautiful, and good. In other words, our inability to understand God or control the universe doesn't change the fact that He is good and in control.

God can cause you, like the eagle, to soar in your life and to be exalted to high places. Even though His methods may be difficult to understand and sometimes hard to endure, God has a proven track record of caring for His creatures. We have only to look at the animal kingdom to see that this is so. God cares for the animal kingdom, not out of duty, but out of love of His creation.

And, do you know what? He loves you far more.

God Will Sustain You Through Suffering

"How can I trust God?" you might find yourself asking when you get another bit of bad news. The test results are back, and they aren't what you prayed for. The phone rings, and you didn't get that job. Your car and your refrigerator break down on the same day. Your son is using again. Another month has passed and you're not pregnant.

Despite your prayers, your trusting, your belief that God will set things right, things just get worse. How do you keep trusting? How do you move forward? How can you keep from giving up and letting go of your faith in God?

When you feel alone and in a barren place, scrabbling to survive, remember that God sustains the wild goats on the barest of mountains. When you feel that your life is spinning out of your control, remember that God can domesticate even a rhinoceros. When you feel foolish and don't have a clue, remember that God can sustain the ostrich. When you feel weak and afraid, remember that God gave the horse the gift of strength. When you feel hopeless and low, remember that God designed the birds of the air to soar.

He sustains all these creatures, and He will sustain you. Do not panic. Do not fret. Do not wring your hands in worry. Follow whatever the Word has to say on that particular subject, and trust God in all things. Don't be so busy trying to understand and control everything that you don't let God do His job of sustaining and comforting you. It's not your job to keep a death grip on your life and all of its circumstances. It's your job to stop forcing something to happen, to sit back, and to trust God to take care of you.

Application

1. Go to God for Your Needs

Do you need strength in your life? Seek God for it. Do you need courage in your life? Seek God for that. Are you looking for beauty? God has the ability to produce that in your soul. Do you want the ability to rise above the problems and the challenges of your life and soar like an eagle? God is the one whom you should seek. These things are His to give.

2. Trust God's Wisdom

Do not panic or complain when God's program does not make sense to you. You need to trust that God is working and that He knows what He is doing. The Creator of the Universe is more than able to handle your life.

If you've been trusting in your job, your money, your health, your education, your marriage, your friends, your family, or your possessions to care for you, God might just allow you to go through a season of adversity in order to reset Himself as King of your life.

3. Review God's Resumé

When you feel yourself questioning God's goodness, it's time to go back and review His resumé. It's throughout the Bible, but Job 38–41 is a great place to revisit. God listed out His qualifications to remind Job that He will sustain His creation. Fire whatever else you hired to care for you, and let God take this position in your life.

Do you trust God to care for you, or are you expecting someone else to meet your needs? My friend, no one else has the resumé of the Creator and Sustainer of the Universe.

Chapter Eight Questions

Question: In Job 39, God listed different animals and how caring for them reveals different aspects of His nature. To which description of these animals do you most relate?

_____

_____

_____

_____

_____

_____

_____

_____

_____

_____

Question: Based on your answer to the previous question, how does your ability to relate to the description of that animal correlate to what God wants to teach you about His character?

_____

_____

_____

_____

_____

_____

_____

_____

_____

_____

Action: Set apart a day (or weekend, if you can) to spend time refocusing on and connecting with God. During this time, make it your aim to 1) go to God with your needs, 2) seek out and commit to trusting God's wisdom, and 3) review God's resumé. Invest in this time with the goal of becoming more confident in God as the Sustainer of the Universe and of your soul.

Chapter Eight Notes

CONCLUSION

God Has a Plan

There's a book called *The Hiding Place*, written by a Dutch woman named Corrie ten Boom.[6] During the Nazi invasion, Corrie and her family hid Jews in their home. A neighbor betrayed them, and Corrie and her sister Betsie were sent to a concentration camp. There, Betsie eventually died. Yet, throughout this horrible season of great suffering, Corrie did not abandon her faith in God.

No, you probably won't face something that extreme. However, I think that Corrie ten Boom's story mirrors Job's. She was living a presumably comfortable life, and then the Nazis came with an evil agenda. She lost her family, her health, and her belongings. Afterward, Corrie wrote about her experiences and became an international figure.

And though things got easier for Corrie, I doubt that she stopped missing Betsie. Corrie was terribly scarred by what happened to her.

As we read through chapter 42 of the book of Job, I think it's easy for us to dismiss Job's suffering. God restored his wealth, his health, and his flocks, and gave him ten new children. Still, Job had to carry the grief for his first ten children. He remembered vividly, I'm sure, the pain of his illness and the hopeless frustration he had felt.

Your time in the School of Patience will come to an end. It will not be eternal. However, you will carry with you the scars you gained there. In the same way, you will carry the lessons you learned there, too. You'll have new empathy for those who are suffering. You will be able to put on your eternal perspective and wait patiently as God works. You won't panic when trouble strikes. Instead, when you find yourself in a dark place, you'll know to put your trust in God. And, above all, you'll know that you have a mediator and savior in Jesus Christ.

Before his trials, Job was said to be a good man. However, when trouble hit, a lot of wrong attitudes and beliefs were revealed in his heart. Job had faulty expectations of God, believing that He was going to go on making Job's life easy because he was a good man.

I'm thankful that God put the final chapter in the book of Job. God brought this man's trials to a close. He also had a purpose for Job's suffering—it was more than just a whim that let this hardship happen. Job needed his heart cleansed, his pride deflated, and his understanding of God reoriented.

All of this is like a documentary made for us on the School of Patience. Suffering is going to happen in the life of every follower of Christ, and the God of the universe has a plan to use it to His eternal benefit and yours. This is the core belief of patience: God is at work, and I will trust in Him.

Have hope in your trials, my friend. Trust that God knows what He is doing. Allow the pain of this process to reveal the deep sin issues hidden in your heart. Know that God's tender mercy is ready and available to restore you to a right relationship with Him.

Don't waste your time complaining; focus on learning. Learn the lessons the School of Patience wants to teach you. Spend time in the Word and in prayer. Listen in church, to wise friends, and to good teaching.

Be humble. Stop trying to be the one calling all the shots. You're shooting in the dark, my friend; it's time to put the gun down. When you find yourself in the midst of adversity and start falling back into old sin patterns, humbly confess and repent. Monitor what is coming out of your mouth, because it is revealing the truth of what is in your heart. Acknowledge that you don't know where you are on the map, and let someone else lead you out of the maze.

Christian, take hope that the darkened road on which you find yourself has a designed destination. Even though it does not look like it right now, God is taking you somewhere good.

Why should we rejoice when we fall into trials and temptations? Because God says you are gaining patience. Patience does not fix all of my problems. Rather, it enables me to walk through them with cheerful endurance. Patience is about learning to trust God, even when we do not understand Him.

About the Author

Joe Dickinson was born in Oklahoma City, Oklahoma, and graduated from Plainview High School in Ardmore, Oklahoma. As a five-year-old child, while attending a church in Ardmore, Joe accepted Christ. Being called to ministry shortly thereafter, he attended and graduated from Heartland Baptist Bible College with a bachelor's degree in biblical studies. In 2011, he received a Master of Arts in Religion from Liberty Baptist Theological Seminary.

He has been married to his wife, Tisha, since 2003, and they now have four children. A year after they got married, Joe was called to be on staff at Hillcrest Baptist Church in El Paso, Texas, as the youth pastor. Since that time, Joe has served in multiple capacities, including as the associate pastor and music director. In 2009, Joe was called to be the pastor of Hillcrest Baptist Church, where he still serves today.

About Sermon To Book

SermonToBook.com began with a simple belief: that sermons should be touching lives, *not* collecting dust. That's why we turn sermons into high-quality books that are accessible to people all over the globe.

Turning your sermon series into a book exposes more people to God's Word, better equips you for counseling, accelerates future sermon prep, adds credibility to your ministry, and even helps make ends meet during tight times.

John 21:25 tells us that the world itself couldn't contain the books that would be written about the work of Jesus Christ. Our mission is to try anyway. Because in heaven, there will no longer be a need for sermons or books. Our time is now.

If God so leads you, we'd love to work with you on your sermon or sermon series.

Visit www.sermontobook.com to learn more.

REFERENCES

Notes

1. Jeremiah, David. *When Your World Falls Apart: Seeing Past the Pain of the Present.* Thomas Nelson Publishers, 2004.

2. Hand, David, dir. *Bambi.* Walt Disney Productions, 1942.

3. Geronimi, Clyde, Wilfred Jackson, and Hamilton Luske, dir. *Cinderella.* Walt Disney Productions, 1950.

4. Lewis, C. S. "Faith." Book 3, ch. 12, in *Mere Christianity.* HarperOne, 1980, p. 144.

5. Avildsen, John G., dir. *The Karate Kid.* Columbia Pictures, 1984.

6. ten Boom, Corrie. *The Hiding Place.* Chosen Books, 1971.

Made in the USA
Columbia, SC
03 August 2024

39541002R00080